Landscape: Poems

Manuel José Othón

Landscape: Poems

Edited and Translated By
Alexander J. McNair

Cenzontle Books
Waco, Texas
2021

Prologue, Selection, Translation, Notes
Copyright © 2021 by Alexander J. McNair

First Edition

All rights reserved.

Landscape: Poems
by Manuel José Othón (1858-1906)
Edited and Translated by Alexander J. McNair
    English and Spanish Text
    Includes bibliographical references

Cover Painting: José María Velasco (1840-1912), "Valle de México, 1888" / Wikimedia Commons / Public Domain
Author Illustration: Digitization of sketch by Julio Ruelas (1870-1907), originally published in Manuel José Othón, *Poemas rústicos* (México, DF: Aguilar Vera y Cía, Editores, 1902) / Public Domain
Illustrations on pages 42, 60, 88, 120: digitized and filtered from Julio Ruelas, illus., *Poemas escogidos* by M.J. Othón (México, DF: Cultura, 1917) / Public Domain

Library of Congress Subject Heading:
    Mexican poetry—19th century
LOC Author/Creator:
    Othón, Manuel José, 1858-1906 (PQ 7297.O79)

ISBN: 978-0-578-90342-2

Cenzontle Books
2021

To Mom,
because Aunt Rebecca would have loved this

Contents

Prologue 09
Surgite! 19
Voz interna/Inner Voice 25
Crepúsculos/Twilights 31
Paisajes/Landscapes 37
Lobreguez/Gloom 43
Ocaso 52
Sunset 53
Nostálgica/Nostalgic 55
Himno de los bosques/Hymn of the Woods 61
I 62
II 64
III 66
IV 70
V 74
VI 78
VII 82
La montaña 86
Mountain 87
Pastoral 89
I 90
II 94
III 98
IV 100
V 104
VI 106
VII 108
VIII 112
IX 116
X 118
En el desierto. Idilio salvaje/In the Desert. Wild Idyll 121
Notes 137
References 147
About the Author 151

Prologue

"Here, Painter, is your splendid landscape": the opening of Manuel José Othón's poem "Sunset."[1] In Spanish, the word for landscape is *paisaje*, which the *Diccionario de la lengua española* (2001) defines thus:

1. extensión de terreno que se ve desde un sitio
2. extensión de terreno considerada en su aspecto artístico
3. pintura o dibujo que representa cierta extensión de terreno

The first three definitions of the word "Landscape" in *Webster's New World Dictionary of the American Language* (1960) could almost be a mirror image of the Spanish entry for *paisaje*:

1. a picture representing a section of natural inland scenery, as of prairie, woodland, mountains, etc.
2. the branch of painting, photography, etc. dealing with such pictures
3. an expanse of natural scenery seen by the eye in one view

The English dictionary entry is not an "exact" translation, if such a thing is possible. Like the reflection of a mountain on the rippling surface of a lake, the definitions reflect but also distort the Spanish entry. The first definition in Spanish corresponds roughly to the third one in *Webster's*: an expanse (or *extensión*) of land seen from a single point of view. This is the objective reality from which the Spanish definition takes its next two meanings: (2) that same expanse of land considered artistically; and (3) a painting or drawing that represents a certain expanse of land. English begins with the definition of "landscape" as a work of art (corresponding roughly to the third Spanish definition), while both English and Spanish have, as their second definitions, "landscape" as the object of art or artistic expression. Here are the three uses of the word in one sentence, followed by the number of the

English definition in parenthesis: "The painter, a specialist in the art of *landscape* (2), painted this *landscape* (1), which represents that *landscape* (3)." Just such a sentence could be written in Spanish with the word *paisaje* (reversing only the numbers 1 and 3).

Reading Othón's poem, then, we have to ask what he means when he points out the *paisaje*/landscape to his dedicatee, "a painter." Is he indicating a specific view or scene while gazing out into nature with the painter, as in "this is a landscape worth painting"? Or is he standing before a painting, admiring the artist's handy work, in which case the poem is an exercise in *ekphrasis*? There is no "there, you should paint that" in the poem to let us know, definitively, which meaning of the word he intends. The poem, a sonnet, walks us through the elements of this landscape, illuminated by the setting sun. The reader can look at the original and translation in this anthology to see how the poet chooses to lay the elements out for his reader, but they are essentially these: a dark lake, gusts of wind, crimson shades, deep blue skies beyond the cloudscape, tree trunk and branches, green hills, and yellow forest floor, stone outcrop covered in lichens, a glimmer of light on a single patch of earth, and in the distance (back to the lake) a sail standing out against the sunset. We, the readers, are eavesdropping on a conversation between the poet and the painter. Where do we situate ourselves? Where do we picture them? On a balcony at sunset? In the artist's studio at midday? Or perhaps this is a landscape remembered, not unlike William Wordsworth's daffodils, which "flash upon that inward eye." I like to think of this poem not as a description of a specific landscape (natural view or painting) but as an invitation to imagine one for ourselves. Othón, in this and many poems, teaches us how to "see" the landscape unfold before our eyes as we read. The poem is also, though it seems to instruct the painter, a demonstration of how to make a poem at the end of the nineteenth century; an *arte poética*, if you will.

Two decades after Othón wrote this poem, the Chilean poet Vicente Huidobro would pen his own *Arte poética*, an eighteen-line avante-garde manifesto in which he challenged his fellow poets not to sing of roses, but to make them bloom: "Por qué cantáis la rosa, ¡oh poetas! / hacedla florecer en el poema."[2] Easier said than done. Huidobro would have chafed under the restrictions of a form like the sonnet, but Othón's work does indeed "invent new worlds," as Huidobro's manifesto insists: it reflects the awesome (beautiful, but sometimes terrifying) forces of nature he sees, allowing the reader to experience that awe in the imagination—even if Othón does so with more adjectives than Huidobro would have approved. For Huidobro, the "poet is a little god"; while Othón sees the poet's job as recreating some small part of the wonder of God's creation. Where Huidobro insists on the poet's creative powers (*creacionismo*, "creationism," the movement he tried to spawn), Othón engages the reader in acts of "recreation": "to refresh or restore in body or mind" but also "to create anew" (according to Webster). One of my motivations for returning to the art and poetry of late nineteenth-century landscape is to recreate the experience of pleasure we have in standing before these canvases, in allowing ourselves to be absorbed by the artist's vision. On landscape art in nineteenth-century Mexico and the United States, Octavio Paz wrote that "painters combined a predilection for visual, almost photographic exactitude and an affection for the vast open spaces of earth, sea, and sky." In the case of a painter like José María Velasco, however, there was an interest not just in "reproducing" nature photographically, the specifically "Mexican" landscape, but in typifying that landscape in such a way that the "essence" of Mexico becomes present to the viewer. Paz continues: "there is a constant note in nineteenth-century landscape painting, in Europe as well as America, that disappears with Impressionism: the attraction of the infinite. In these painters the precision of detail is allied to a sublime vision of nature."[3] We can appreciate this when we see mankind's diminutive stature in the sweeping vistas of Velasco's series of landscapes on the Valley of Mexico (such as the one from 1888 on our cover); Mexico City is a *mancha* (or stain) in the distance, on the plain before the normally soaring peaks of Popocatépetl and Iztaccíhuatl, which themselves appear to be dwarfed by the sky and cloudscape; the era's most advanced technology—the steam engine locomotive—is nothing but a puff of smoke. Reading Othón's lyric sequence "Pastoral" is a lot like walking through a gallery full of landscape paintings.

Manuel José Othón (1858-1906) was born in San Luis Potosí, north of Mexico City by more than 200 miles, and would die there forty-eight years later, though he moved quite a bit among the small towns and cities of north central Mexico as a lawyer and judge.[4] He was on his way from Mexico City to his home in Durango in late 1906 when his health began to fail. He stopped in San Luis Potosí and sent for his wife, knowing the end was near. As Jorge Luis Borges would write, perhaps ironically, in his famous story "El sur" (The South): "Reality is partial to symmetries and slight anachronisms." Othón's life and work seem to make this point. He grew up in a time of great upheaval, armed revolts, but he retreated to a classical education. Many poets of the mid-nineteenth century had been swept up in the "exaltation, passion, rebellion" of the Romantic movement, which found its voice in Mexico with poets such as Manuel Acuña, but Othón found inspiration in Virgil and Horace.[5] He was not completely unaware of the literary movements of his day (as a young man, he translated and adapted the great Romantics—Lord Byron, Victor Hugo, Gustavo Adolfo Bécquer—and he read the Spanish American modernists—Gutiérrez Nájera, Darío, Lugones, etc.—from the late-1880s onward), but he dedicated as much time to Dante, Cervantes, and Fray Luis de León. He has been described as a "modern bucolic poet," but "he in no way resembles the artificial pastoral poets or pasteboard singers of nature who worked with a classical yardstick."[6] Othón began writing poems at an early age and was so devoted to the craft of poetry that it distracted him from Law, his official course of study at the Instituto Científico de San Luis. One of his biographers, Jesús Zavala, relates that his fiancee, Josefa Jiménez, broke off their engagement at one point in an effort to inspire him to finish his degree.[7] He published his first volume of poetry, *Poesías*, in 1880; he received his diploma to practice law in December 1881; he and Josefa were married on February 5, 1883, after a five-year engagement.

Another book of poems, *Nuevas poesías*, followed that same year (1883) and Othón continued to write short fiction and plays throughout his life, but would not publish another book of poetry until almost twenty years later. After writing more than eighty poems between 1876 and 1883, he wrote barely a dozen between 1883 and 1890. In 1884 the newlyweds spent a couple of months in Mexico City before Othón began a series of appointments to provincial judgeships. Every few years they would move back to San Luis Potosí for a time (1891-1893, for example, he taught at the Instituto Científico). By 1892 his early poetry along with his continued writing of fiction, drama and criticism had earned him an election to the Academia Mexicana de la Lengua. The 1890s brought him a renewed interest in cultivating poetry and his poems began appearing with more frequency in local periodicals as well as international magazines such as *Revista Azul* and *Revista Moderna*, both of which were major vehicles for the dissemination of modernist poetry and prose. Othón collected the poems he had composed or revised between 1889 and 1901 into a new book, *Poemas rústicos* (1902), which he published in Mexico City and dedicated to the city of Guadalajara. He had never lived in Guadalajara or the state of Jalisco, but serving as a *diputado suplente* (something like an alternate for congressmen) in 1900, Othón represented Jalisco in the chamber of *diputados* in Mexico City after their regular representative became indisposed. Several of his poems in the 1890s had also appeared in Guadalajara journals. The first edition of *Poemas rústicos* had a print run of 500 copies.

Despite the title (*Rustic poems*), Othón was not writing for an uncultured audience. In his prologue to the reader he claimed that the artist had to be sincere to the point of naivety, but that Art itself ought to be accessible only to a few "espíritus finos" (refined spirits), already sensitized to aesthetic appreciation. Othón exalted Art to the status of religion: Art is Beauty and Truth, "one of the most powerful links to eternal Truth and infinite beauty."[8] And he considered the artist's vocation a sacred one: it is not "a pastime or leisure activity, the artist must consecrate all the energy of his heart, mind and life to it."[9] These attitudes place him squarely within the spirit of Spanish American *Modernismo*, though he is careful to distinguish himself from that movement as well. Othón writes that he has spent the previous twenty years trying to shake off "outside" influences—a reference to the modernist penchant for seeking French models in its renovation of Spanish poetic language? "The Muse must not be," he claims, "a strange spirit that comes from outside to make an impression on us, but rather must sprout from within ourselves so that, when feeling her in our presence, in contact with Nature, dazzling, loving and caring, we might exclaim in the sacred delight of wonder and ecstasy, as the father of humankind before his divine and eternal bride: *bone of my bones, flesh of my flesh!*"[10] The "contact with Nature" is key for Othón. The previous year (October 26, 1901), Othón had written a letter to the artist Juan B. Delgado, in part responding to Delgado's dismissive review of Salvador Díaz Mirón's collection *Lascas* (Jalapa, 1901). In the letter Othón defends Díaz Mirón's poetic vision and rejects the notion that he is simply moving in the direction of Darío and Lugones (the Latin American modernists). Key for Othón is Díaz Mirón's "regionalist" flavor. The poet of Veracruz, like Othón, is not interested in exotic perfumes and places, the ruins of the Parthenon, the mythical recreations of the modernists, with their faun-filled forests and centaurs bathing in crystal springs. Othón writes of Díaz Mirón's verse "Allí todo es México, más aún, es Veracruz" (There everything is Mexico, even more so Veracruz).[11]

We could easily replace "Veracruz" with San Luis Potosí and the phrase would be an apt description of Othón's later work. Both Díaz Mirón and Othón in that period (c. 1900) had left behind the romantic influences of Byron and Hugo, though there was still a tinge of Baudelairean sickness. In Othón, even more so than in the work of Díaz Mirón, we find idylls, eclogues, and well-sculpted odes; but their natural surroundings are not Arcadian, they are identifiably Mexican. And the environment is not edenic, it is realistic; Othón used the adjective "naturalist" to describe Díaz Mirón's late poetry. When we see the title "Idilio," for example, we might expect "a simple, pleasant scene of rural, pastoral, or domestic life" (*Webster's*), but Díaz Mirón tells us the site is disagreeable: fetid and rough, full of cactus and stinging nettle, cow dung, mud and swarming flies.[12] Likewise, Othón does not flinch from the sometimes harsh realities of the north central highlands of Mexico, where sub-tropical forests meet jagged mountains and give way to arid plains. They are not just a backdrop for human drama; the clashing climes *are* the drama, man is the spectator. In long lyric sequences such as "Hymn of the Woods" or "Pastoral," Othón directs his reader's attention to the most minute details, but also presents the majesty of the landscape. As in the landscape paintings of Velasco, humanity shrinks before the vastness of mountain, plain, and sky: a speck on the horizon, or a precarious building, always on the verge of being absorbed back into nature, absorbing us as we take it all in. Antonio Castro Leal described it this way: "His [Othón's] nature was American nature, with traces of cataclysm and Tertiary landslides, where weighty blocks of fantastic geometry sculpt a majestic and rough landscape, frightening and awe-inspiring; where the sun of four ages has scorched the shining deserts and their receding horizons; where immense, uncontainable, devastating waters, murky with sand, have drilled through mountain ranges, leaving their memory behind in caves, canyons, and ravines. A nature of majestic, soaring stones, dense tropical forests, lit up by lightning bolts and resounding with thunder, storm and flood."[13]

Latin American poets had taken up the description of this dramatic, American, landscape before Othón, of course, but always in the interest of more human concerns. For Andrés Bello (1781-1865), the landscape portrayed in "Agriculture in the Torrid Zone" is the object of patriotic pride and human potential. For José María Heredia (1803-1839), the hurricanes, cataracts, and vast wildernesses of the western hemisphere are always a reflection of his own longings or an invitation to philosophize (not unlike the English countryside was for Wordsworth).[14] By contrast, Othón, especially in his later poems, merely paints the landscape; he does not interpret it. He allows his reader to experience the wonder of nature, in all its violence and beauty, where man has left only a tiny, pitiful mark on the landscape. This renegotiation of mankind's role in the natural universe—to nature's advantage—right on the cusp of the twentieth century, seems to cry out for an Ecocritical response. But Othón's approach, like the shepherd of his pastoral, is a lone voice in the wilderness of modern Latin American letters. The Uruguayan writer Mario Benedetti, commenting on the theme of nature in Latin American literature, notes that there has been a reaction in contemporary poetry against the nineteenth century's reverence for nature: "la parquedad con que los poetas actuales asumen el paisaje se convierte en un acto estéticamente subversivo" (the scarcity with which current poets take up the landscape has become an aesthetically subversive act). As a result, the landscapes of Othón and Heredia, in light of contemporary aesthetics, seem more distant than Homer.[15]

Othón's standing among readers and critics has had its ups and downs over the last century. In his prologue to a 1917 edition of Othón's selected poems, Agustín Loera y Chávez wrote with admiration that Othón was "el más grande cantor de la naturaleza en este país" (the greatest singer of nature in this country).[16] Three decades after the poet's pre-mature death, the critic Isaac Goldberg could still recognize Othón as "one of the six great Mexican moderns."[17] Twenty years after that, however, Octavio Paz would complain that Othón made "no attempt at innovation in his work."[18] For Paz, working in the wake of the *Modernismo* against which contemporary Latin America poetry defined itself in the mid-twentieth century, only Othón's sonnet sequence *Idilio salvaje* (Wild Idyll) redeems him from the unremarkable waste bin of late-nineteenth-century "academic tradition." José Emilio Pacheco appears to share Paz's opinion. Pacheco includes Othón in his anthology of Spanish-American modernism, but writes that "his entire body of work seems a stylistic exercise for the writing of *Wild Idyll*."[19] While the poet still has a place in Pacheco's anthology and in the canon of Mexican poetry, Othón has all but disappeared from general anthologies of Latin American literature. Antonio Castro Leal, in his edition of Othón's poetry and short story, laments that "of all the great Mexican poets, Manuel José Othón is the least read and also the least appreciated; outside of Mexico he is barely known."[20]

This descent into obscurity is partly a function of *Modernismo*'s outsized role in Spanish-American literary history. Its importance as the first truly Latin American literary movement (i.e. exported from Latin America, rather than imported to it as Romanticism, Neoclassicism, and the Baroque were previously) has never really been in question. But modernist poetry itself is undergoing something of a rehabilitation among critics, after a century of reactions against it. Othón's poetry, though it was overlooked (or dismissed) by mid-century critics and poets, in their efforts to distance themselves from *Modernismo*, has not been rehabilitated with the other modernists in more recent days. His work, in words Borges might have used, was a "slight anachronism"; he was just a little out of synch with the movement that defined his generation. Uneasy among the modernists, Othón was critical of the "South American poets" along with Mexican poets—Amado Nervo and José Juan Tablada, for example—who would follow them: "everything is conventionalism, affectation, obsession with being unique; there is nothing sincere or spontaneous, though at times they do exquisite work."[21] Othón's work exalts a specifically Mexican landscape, while the modernists often sought out exotic locales or mythic dreamscapes in their efforts to project sophistication and cosmopolitanism. Yet Othón was neither a classical (i.e., academic) throwback nor a romantic holdover, as detractors have averred. Carlos González Peña wrote of "the complexity of his literary personality": if Othón was "by education and literary tastes, a classicist; by temperament he was something more than a romanticist: he was a modern."[22] Among the second generation modernist poets of Mexico, Luis G. Urbina was enthusiastic about Othón's poetry, calling it "a manual of truth, of energy, of life's feeling"; Urbina thought Othón's works, "carved in marble," would be "among those that endure."[23]

The landscape painter, José María Velasco, and the landscape poet, Manuel José Othón, have been overshadowed by their modernist and avante-garde successors. Velasco and Othón perfected an art and a genre, landscape, which changing aesthetics would soon question, and then upend. Huidobro, for example, in his poem "Paisaje" pokes fun at the conventions of landscape painting and its aficionados in galleries and museums. It is a "concrete" poem meant to imitate the layout of a landscape painting. Where the viewer of a painting might expect to see a tree in the frame (or on the page), Huidobro writes "El árbol / era más alto / que la / montaña" (the tree was taller than the mountain). To the left he has text describing a mountain, to the right and trailing off toward the bottom of the page he has the lines "El / río / que / corre / no lleva / peces" (the running river carries no fish). In the upper right-hand corner the text forms a circle, indicating the moon "where you gaze upon yourself." The text at the bottom of the page warns viewers to stay off the freshly painted grass.[24] Clever. The art historian Fausto Ramírez has written that José María Velasco "was a victim of that—by all accounts cruel yet unavoidable—generational changing of the guard, which affects, among many other things, artistic tastes."[25] So too with Othón, though there is much still to admire in his work. We can be jaded, cynical in this post-modern era, as we cast our eyes back to the late nineteenth century, but I do not think we can be as flippant as Huidobro was. These landscapes will reward our gaze.

A NOTE ON SELECTION AND TRANSLATION

In selecting poems for this collection I have used many (though not all) of the works predominately about landscape or nature from Othón's *Poemas rústicos* (1902). Not all the poems in the 1902 collection neatly match the theme of landscape, so I have omitted many poems (a bilingual edition of the complete *Poemas rústicos* is a project for the future), but I have respected the order in which the poems appeared in the 1902 edition, the archaic spellings (e.g, *obscuro* for *oscuro*), and the revisions that Othón made there (when they differed from previously published versions). As a result, the poems are arranged here (almost) chronologically by original composition date, so the reader can get a feel for how Othón's own aesthetics were evolving away from the late-Romantic and toward a more unique variant of Modernism. At the end of the present collection I include the seven sonnets from the *Idilio salvaje/Wild Idyll* sequence, written and published after *Poemas rústicos* and among the last poems Othón wrote before his death. Samuel Beckett translated *Wild Idyll* for the anthology of Mexican poetry that he did in collaboration with Octavio Paz in the late-1950s, and I had initially thought to "leave them well enough alone," as they say. But the more I read them, the more they called to me; my readings kept suggesting English lines I could not dismiss. I like the Beckett translations very much, but I couldn't resist making my own. I have documented the major discrepancies between versions in the notes. I have also used the notes to clarify allusions, translate Latin phrases, indicate some of the influences on our poet. Since Othón was a voracious reader, these influences are many. In pastoral or bucolic modes alone, Othón absorbs Virgil and Horace, Garcilaso and Lope de Vega, Heredia and Joaquín Arcadio Pagaza, while also anticipating César Vallejo's "Imperial Nostalgias" or Neruda's "Heights of Macchu Picchu." Bernard Knox, in his preface to *The Norton Book of Classical Literature*, writes "In translation this intertextual depth is inevitably lost; even the overt allusions are often to exotic texts or obscure myths that demand a footnote." He despairs: "translation cannot cope with this."

This bilingual edition is presented in facing-page format, so the reader can enjoy the original and glance over now and again to see how I have chosen to render the lines; but I have translated in verse so that the English version might stand on its own. The reader should know these are not word-for-word renderings. Though I try to be as faithful as possible, I find the "literal" cribs tiresome; prose should only serve as a tool for helping the reader to puzzle out lexical and grammatical difficulties of the original. In making these translations I have tried to imitate the rhythms of the original lines without straying too far from their "sense." As a matter of principle I try to avoid heavy end-stopped rhymes, which if not managed properly in English can have unintended comic effects, but I have not ruled rhyme out completely. Edith Grossman's chapter on translating poetry in *Why Translation Matters* (2010) has helped me to hone my practice in the last few years; it serves as an antidote to the desperation one sometimes feels when engaged in the "impossible" task of translating poems. I am cognizant of the beautiful soundscapes that Othón has left us in his poetry, in the process of conjuring such transcendent visual landscapes. This is one of the reasons I decided to make this a bilingual edition. If my English renderings of his landscapes manage to capture a fraction of Othón's soundscape, I will consider this a success.

Surgite!

I

   Blanco el cielo. Montañas obscuras
se destacan en fondo gris perla.
Sobre el pico más alto ha prendido
su penacho de luz una estrella.
Un alfange de plata la luna,
recortando las nubes, semeja
y un lucero, muy pálido y triste,
desde el negro perfil de la sierra,
somnoliento, su blanca mirada
arrojando, al morir, parpadea;
a la vez que otros astros se ocultan
en el seno de la húmeda niebla.

II

   Los nocturnos ruidos se apagan
y se apagan también las estrellas.
Por el Este sus franjas de oro,
de la aurora gentil mensajeras,
tiende el sol que en su lecho de nubes
como un rey oriental se espereza.
Y las sombras, buscando refugio,
de Occidente en los mares navegan
y el espacio atraviesan veloces,
tripulando sus góndolas negras.
Sólo Venus esplende, vibrando
su mirada imperiosa de reina.

I

  White, the sky. Dark mountains soar
against a backdrop of pearly gray.
Above the highest peak, a star gathers
in its plumed headdress of light.
The moon seems a silver scimitar,
slicing its way through the clouds,
and a planet, sleepy, sad and pale,
just beyond the sierra's black edge,
casting its white gaze toward earth,
blinks twice and then disappears;
and all at once the other orbs vanish
within the bosom of a humid mist.

II

  Nocturnal noises fade away,
and stars too are extinguished.
The sun, like a king of the Orient
stretched out on his bed of clouds,
extends his bands of gold, dawn's
gentle messengers, throughout the East.
And shadows, seeking refuge,
sail the Western seas and, swift,
make their passage through space,
crewing their tar-black skiffs.
Venus alone still shines, her gaze,
imperious as a queen's, shimmering.

III

En la tierra las cosas presienten
un instante solemne, y esperan.
Surte el agua, las fuentes palpitan,
se estremece la obscura arboleda
y entre el hondo temblor de las frondas
laten almas que cantan y vuelan.
Son alados espíritus: brotan
del ramaje; las hojas despliegan
el sutil pabellón de esmeraldas . . .
Todo es vida y calor, todo tiembla
cuando el sol, rosa inmensa de fuego,
su lumínico polen dispersa.

IV

A lo lejos se siente el estruendo
del trabajo y la lucha que llegan.
El reposo es momento que pasa;
perdurable tan sólo es la brega.
¡Hombre, sús! abandona tu lecho
que la vida te llama y espera.
Ya en tu seno las vísceras laten;
ya en tus sienes la sangre golpea.
¡La montaña calcárea, a tus huesos;
sus entrañas de hierro, a tus venas,
y a tu espíritu ardiente los rayos
en que inunda tu Dios las esferas!

III

   Here on the earth all things sense
a solemn moment; and they wait.
Water gushes, the springs pulse,
the dark grove shudders and deep
within the trembling fronds,
the throbbing souls fly and sing.
They are winged spirits: they burst
from the branches; leaves unfurl
a soft pavilion of emerald green . . .
Everything is life and heat, trembling
when the sun, immense rose of fire,
scatters its luminescent pollen.

IV

   In the distance a rumbling is felt:
the coming labor, struggles of the day.
Repose is but a fleeting instant;
toil is the only thing that endures.
Onward, Man! Abandon your bed,
for life calls to you and waits.
Your guts thump at your breast,
and your temples throb with blood.
The mountain's chalk for your bones,
its entrails of iron for your veins,
and for your ardent spirit, the rays
your God employs to flood the spheres!

Voz interna/
Inner Voice

En las noches tediosas y sombrías
buscan su nido en mi cerebro enfermo,
plegando el ala ensangrentada y rota,
mis antiguos recuerdos.
No vienen como alegres golondrinas
de la rústica iglesia a los aleros,
trayendo de la rubia Primavera
las blandas brisas y los tibios besos.
Vienen, como los pájaros nocturnos,
a acurrucarse huraños y siniestros
de la musgosa tapia en las ruinas
o de la vieja torre entre los huecos.

¡Que vengan en buena hora, que no tarden!
¿Por qué no se apresuran? ¡Los espero! . . .
¡Hace ya tantos años que dormito!
¡Hace ya tanto tiempo!
El negro muro del hendido claustro,
aunque roto y abierto,
aun se mantiene en pie, y en las ojivas
del campanario viejo,
si no hay esquilas que a la misa llamen
al asomar el matinal lucero
o anuncien la oración al campesino
y la hora del regreso
a las muchachas de la azul cisterna,
al pastor y al vaquero;
si ya no hay campanitas que repiquen

On tedious and somber nights
those ancient memories of mine
seek out a nest in my infirm brain,
folding a bloody, broken wing.
They don't come like happy swallows
to the eaves of a country church,
bringing the mild breezes and warm
kisses of fair spring. No, they come
instead like nocturnal birds to curl up,
cold-hearted and sinister, in the
moss-covered ruins of the old stone wall
or among the holes of the tower.

   They're welcome to come, let them not delay!
Why don't they hurry? I'm here waiting!
So many years I have been dozing,
so much time already!
The dark wall of the crumbling cloister,
though broken and undone,
is still standing after all, and in the arches
of the old bell tower,
there are no bells tolling for mass
at the rising of the morning star
or announcing prayers for the farmer
or marking the girls' return
from the blue cistern, or end of day
for ranch-hand and shepherd;
even if the church bell no longer tolls

del santo titular en los festejos,
hay oquedades hondas y sombrías
que abrigarán en sus obscuros senos
a las lechuzas pardas y siniestras
y a los pájaros negros . . . .

the feast day of the patron saint,
at least there are deep, shadowy hollows
that will shelter in their dark bosom
the sinister, brown barn owls
and the black birds . . .

Crepúsculos/
Twilights

I

   Rubia la aurora luce en el Oriente
sus galas más espléndidas de fiesta,
que amorosa y rendida ya se apresta
del esposo a besar la roja frente.

   Para verle asomar alza su ingente
tajada cumbre la montaña enhiesta;
prepárale su incienso la floresta,
su trino el ave y su rumor la fuente.

   El cielo gotas de cristal rocía
en corolas y muérdagos. Los vientos
tañen las ramas de la selva umbría.

   Y alza a su Dios en rítmicos acentos,
como grata oración del nuevo día,
himnos la tierra . . . ¡el hombre, pensamientos!

I

  In the Orient rubicund Aurora flaunts
her most splendid festival attire;
lovingly and enthralled, she readies
herself to kiss her husband's red brow.

  To watch him appear, the lofty mountain
raises its enormous, sharpened peak;
the leafy grove prepares its incense for him,
the bird, its song and its murmur, the spring.

  The heavens sprinkle crystal drops
on corollas and mistletoe. Wind strums
on the branches of the forest shade.

  And, as a prayer of thanks for new day,
the earth lifts a hymn of sweet rhythms
to her God . . . and man, his meditations!

II

   Tramonta el sol. Esmalta la colina
de su postrera luz con el escaso
fulgor, que va envolviendo en el Ocaso
con su túnica blanca de neblina.

   Desbarátase la húmeda calina
en la llana extensión del campo raso,
y ya por el Oriente, paso a paso,
la silenciosa noche se avecina.

   Todo es misterio y paz. El tordo canta
sobre los olmos del undoso río;
el hato a los apriscos se adelanta.

   Flota el humo en el pardo caserío
y mi espíritu al cielo se levanta
hasta perderse en Ti . . . ¡Gracias, Dios mio!

II

   The sun glides down the mountain and
glazes the hillside with the scant glow
of its final gleam, which the mist slowly
envelopes with its white tunic: Sunset.

   The moist fog on the vast plain
of open fields begins to break up,
and already out of the Orient, step
by step, the silent night approaches.

   All is mystery and tranquility. The thrush
sings over the elms by the wavy river;
the herd advances toward its pen.

   Smoke floats over the dusty homestead
and my spirit rises to the heavens
until losing itself in You . . . Thank you, My God!

Paisajes/
Landscapes

I

Meridies

  Rojo, desde el cenit, el sol caldea.
La torcaz cuenta al río sus congojas,
medio escondida entre las mustias hojas
que el viento apenas susurrando orea.

  La milpa, ya en sazón, amarillea,
de espigas rebosante y de panojas,
y reverberan las techumbres rojas
en las vecinas casas de la aldea.

  No se oye estremecerse el cocotero
ni en la ribera sollozar los sauces;
solos están la vega y el otero,

  desierto el robledal, secos los cauces
y, tendido a la orilla de un estero,
abre el lagarto sus enormes fauces.

I

Meridies

  The sun smolders red there at its zenith.
The dove recounts her sorrows to the river,
half-hidden among the withered leaves
now dried up by the wind's soft whisper.

  The corn turns yellow, already in season,
field brimming with stalks and ears,
while reddish roofs sparkle on
neighboring houses in the village.

  The trembling of the coconut palm goes
unheard, as does the weeping of the willow
on the river; meadow and hill are alone.

  The oak grove is deserted, the creeks are dry,
and stretched out on the banks of the estuary
the alligator opens his enormous jaws.

II

Noctifer

Todo es cantos, suspiros y rumores.
Agítanse los vientos tropicales
zumbando entre los verdes carrizales,
gárrulos y traviesos en las flores.

Bala el ganado, silban los pastores,
las vacas van mugiendo a los corrales,
canta la codorniz en los maizales
y grita el guacamayo en los alcores.

El día va a morir; la tarde avanza.
Súbito llama a la oración la esquila
de la ruinosa ermita, en lontananza.

Y Venus, melancólica y tranquila,
desde el perfil del horizonte lanza
la luz primera de su azul pupila.

II

Noctifer

   All is song and sighs and murmurs.
Tropical winds stirred up, whirring
through green reeds, are chatty
and mischievous among the flowers.

   The livestock bleats, shepherds whistle,
cows go bellowing to their corrals,
the quail sings in the corn fields
while the macaw squawks in the hills.

   The day is going to die; evening advances.
Suddenly, the bell from the dilapidated
chapel in the distance calls to prayer.

   And Venus, melancholy and tranquil,
from the edge of the horizon casts
the first light from her azure pupil.

Lobreguez/
Gloom

Bajo un cielo plomizo y ventoso,
por aristas de piedra cortado,
el paisaje monótono duerme
en profundo y solemne letargo.
Todo es gris: la silueta del monte,
el inmóvil y frío remanso
que refleja en sus ondas obscuras
un girón sepulcral del espacio;
los barbechos de glebas grietadas
donde yace el rastrojo hacinado,
olvidadas están las coyundas
y descansan los rotos arados;
los corrales de piso fangoso
que han hollado pezuñas y cascos,
sobre el cual, por el aire impelidos,
flotan acres y fétidos vahos;
el humilde jacal del labriego,
mal envuelto en los grises andrajos
que el aliento de Otoño arrebata
del humoso fogón solitario;
el derruido y vetusto convento
de sillares musgosos y pardos,
otro tiempo de monjes refugio
y hoy albergue de espectros y cárabos;
hasta el río de gárrulas ondas
y cristales bullentes y claros,
so las húmedas nieblas, yacente
hoy está, moribundo y helado.

   Beneath the windy, leaden sky,
pierced by ridges of stone,
the monotonous landscape sleeps
in deep and solemn lethargy.
All is gray: the mount's silhouette,
the pool, still and cold, reflecting
in its lugubrious waves the great
sepulchral spiral of space;
the fallow fields cracked with clods
where the stubble stacks lie,
and the forgotten yokes stay,
and the broken plows find rest;
the corrals with the muddy ground,
trodden by horseshoe and hoof,
where the acrid, fetid vapors float,
before they are driven through the air;
the humble laborer's hut, wrapped
poorly in the gray rags that
Autumn's breath has snatched
from the smoky, solitary stove;
the ancient convent in ruins
with its brown, moss-covered stone,
at one time a refuge for monks,
today it shelters specters and owls;
even the river with its normally garrulous
waves and crystals seething yet clear,
beneath the humid mist today
is now moribund, frozen, and still.

Ya lobrece. Las sombras nocturnas,
como espesa humareda, borrando
van el triste confín de Occidente
con un negro y furioso brochazo.
Zumba el Bóreas; los vientos aúllan
remolinos de polvo aventando
y barriendo las nubes que corren
en tropel tumultoso y fantástico.
La hojarasca crepita dispersa
por las calles tortuosas del rancho,
do se ve agonizar un destello
tras los viejos postigos cerrados.
Y se escucha, a la vez, el chasquido
de las ramas crujiendo en el árbol
y el pesado caer de las gotas
en las áridas sendas del campo.
Las tinieblas se cuajan. El ciclo
doloroso, en un círculo trágico
va ciñendo del torvo paisaje
los perfiles y el hórrido espacio.

A gloom abides. Nocturnal shadows
like a thick cloud of smoke erase
the sad limits of the setting sun
with an angry, black stroke of the brush.
Boreas blows from the north; winds howl
lifting whirlwinds of dust in the air
and sweeping the clouds that run
in a fantastic and tumultuous mob.
The fallen leaves crackle and scatter
through the winding roads of the ranch,
where you can see a glimmer's final
agony behind the old, closed shutters.
And you can hear, simultaneously,
the snap of the cracking branches
in the tree and the heavy drops falling
on the arid paths of the country.
The shadows clot. The mournful sky
surrounds the silhouettes of this
baleful panorama inside a tragic
circle: the horrid void of space.

El relámpago azul fosforesce
una cárdena herida trazando…
en la lóbrega nube, que se abre
al sentir el feroz latigazo;
y en las sombras que envuelven y ciñen
valle y bosques, montañas y llanos,
va a clavar, a intervalos, furente
sus sangrientos puñales el rayo.
Todo es negro: la noche profunda
va extendiendo sus alas de cárabo
y el terror culebrea en los nervios,
el cabello y la piel erizando.
A lo lejos, al fin de la senda
que se incrusta en los duros peñascos,
donde empieza a afilar la montaña
sus aristas de pórfido y cuarzo,
empotradas en la áspera roca
y asomándose al hondo barranco,
sus ruinosas paredes levanta
el humilde rural camposanto.

The blue bolt phosphoresces,
tracing a livid wound over
the gloomy cloud, that opens wide
when it feels the lash of the whip;
and in the shadows wrapping, girding
valley and woods, mountains and plains,
the lightning flash stabs furiously
at intervals with its bloody daggers.
All is black: the night profound
spreads its wings of horned owl
and terror snakes through the nerves,
raising flesh and standing hair on end.
In the distance, at the end of the trail
that makes its way through the stone
crags, where the mountain starts
to hone its edge of porphyry and quartz,
embedded in the harsh rock
and overlooking the deep ravine,
the humble, rural cemetery
raises its now crumbling walls.

En la lúgubre noche, las hienas,
espantoso festín husmeando,
el silencio de muerte profanan
con aullido espasmódico y largo.
A través de los rotos sepulcros,
en la lívida faz de los cráneos
¡con qué horror, con qué horror aparece
terrorífica mueca de espanto!
Tal vez sienten la garra acercarse,
y allí están, impotentes y trágicos . . .
¡Y del mundo, y del cielo, y del alma
olvidados, oh, Dios, olvidados!

In the lugubrious night, the hyenas
sniff around the frightful feast,
profaning the silence of death
with their long, spasmodic howls.
Through broken sepulchers, on
the pallid surface of skulls
—such horror, such horror appears
in their dreadful expression of fear!
Perhaps they sense the claw approach,
and there they are, powerless and tragic . . .
and forgotten by the world, and by heaven,
and by the soul, oh God, forgotten!

Ocaso

A un pintor

He aquí, pintor, tu espléndido paisaje:
un lago obscuro, ráfagas marinas
empapadas en tintas cremesinas
y en el azul profundo del celaje;

un tronco que columpia su ramaje
al soplo de las auras vespertinas
y manchadas de verde de las colinas
y de amarillo el fondo del boscaje;

un peñasco de líquenes cubierto;
una faja de tierra iluminada
por el último rayo del sol muerto;

y, de la tarde al resplandor escaso,
una vela a lo lejos, anegada
en la divina calma del ocaso.

Sunset

To a painter

Here, Painter, is your splendid landscape:
a darkened lake, gusts from the sea
soaked in shades of crimson, and
deepest azure of the cloud break;

a trunk swinging its branches to
the blowing of the evening breeze
and the hills stained with green
and the thicket floor, a yellow hue;

a stone outcrop covered in lichens;
a patch of earth illuminated
by the dying sun's last ray of light;

and, in the twilight's sparing gleam,
a sail in the distance, bathed
in the divine calm of the setting sun.

Nostálgica/ Nostalgic

O, ubi campi!

En estos días tristes y nublados
en que pesa la niebla sobre mi alma
cual una losa sepulcral, ¡ay! cómo
mis ojos se dilatan
tras esos limitados horizontes
que cierran las montañas,
queriendo penetrar otros espacios,
cual en un mar sin límites ni playas.
¡Pobre pájaro muerto por el frío!
¿Para qué abandonaste tus campañas,
tu cielo azul, tus fértiles praderas
y viniste a morir entre la escarcha?

¡Oh, mi naturaleza azul y verde!
¿Dónde están tus profundas lontananzas
en que otros días engolfé mi vista
anhelante de sombras y de ráfagas?
¿Dónde están tus arroyos bullidores,
tus negras y espantosas hondonadas
que poblaron mi espíritu de ensueños
o a los hondos abismos lo arrojaban?

He de morir. Mas, ¡ay! que no mi vida
se apague entre estas brumas. La tenaza
del odio, de la envidia el corvo diente
y el venenoso aliento de las almas
por la corte oprimidas, aquí sólo
podránme dar, al fin de la jornada,
la desesperación más que la muerte,
¡y yo quiero la muerte triste y pálida!

In these sad and cloudy days
in which the fog presses in on my soul
like the sepulchral stone,
oh, how my eyes stretch
beyond those limited horizons
closed in by the mountains,
wanting to penetrate other spaces
like a sea without limits or shores!
Wretched bird killed by the cold!
Why did you abandon your fields,
your azure sky, your fertile meadows
to come and die among the frosts?

   O my green and sky-blue country,
where are your vast open spaces,
which at other times absorbed my gaze,
longing, as I did, for wind and shade?
Where are your babbling brooks,
your dark, appalling hollows, which
filled my spirit with imagination or
hurled it toward bottomless abysses?

   I must die. But, oh, don't let my life
burn out among these mists. The pincer
of hate, the curved tooth of envy,
and the venomous breath of souls
oppressed by the city, here at the end
of the day, will only be able to offer
despair, desperation more than death,
and I want sad and pallid death!

Y allá en tus verdes bosques, madre mía,
bajo tu cielo azul, madre adorada,
podré morir al golpe de un peñasco
descuajado de la áspera montaña;
o derrumbarme desde la alta cima,
donde crecen los pinos, y las águilas
viendo de frente al sol labran el nido
y el corvo pico entre las grietas clavan,
hasta el fondo terrible de un barranco
donde me arrastren con furor tus aguas.
Quiero morir allá: que me triture
el cráneo un golpe de tus fuertes ramas
que, por el ronco viento retorcidas,
formen, al distenderse, ruda maza;
o bien, quiero sentir sobre mi pecho
de tus fieras los dientes y las garras,
madre naturaleza de los campos,
de cielo azul y espléndidas montañas.

  Y si quieres que muera poco a poco,
tienes pantanos de aguas estancadas...
¡Infíltrame en las venas el mortífero
hálito pestilente de tus aguas!

And there in your green woods, mother of mine,
beneath your blue skies, beloved mother,
I can die with the blow from a falling stone
dislodged from your harsh mountain;
or tumble down from the highest peak,
there where the pines grow, and the eagles
staring into the sun build their nests
and stab their curved beaks among cracks,
down into the terrible depths of a ravine,
where the fury of your waters will drag me away.
I want to die there: may my skull be crushed
by a blow from your sturdy branches,
which, gnarled by hoarse winds,
bulge out to form a crude hammer;
or better yet, I want to feel on my breast
the teeth and claws of your wild beasts,
Mother Nature, mother of the fields,
of the blues skies and splendid mountains.

And if you want me to die ever so slowly,
you have the marshes with stagnant waters . . .
Filter into my veins the death-bringing,
pestilential vapor rising from your wetland.

Himno de los bosques/
Hymn of the Woods

I

  En este sosegado apartamiento,
lejos de cortesanas ambiciones,
libre curso dejando al pensamiento,
quiero escuchar suspiros y canciones.
¡El himno de los bosques! Lo acompaña
con apacible susurrar el viento,
el coro de las aves con su acento,
con su rumor eterno la montaña.
El torrente caudal se precipita
a la honda sima, con furor azota
las piedras de su lecho, y la infinita
estrofa ardiente de los antros brota.
¡Del gigante salterio en cada nota
el salmo inmenso del amor palpita!

I

   In this peaceful retreat,
far from courtly ambitions,
letting my thoughts run free,
I want to listen to sighs and songs.
The hymn of the woods! The wind
accompanies it with its gentle whisper,
as does the choir of birds with their voices,
and the mountain with its eternal sound.
The great river torrent falls upon
the deep chasm below, lashing
the stones of its bed with fury, and infinite
stanzas burst passionately from their dens.
The immense psalm of love pulses
in every note from that enormous psaltery.

II

Huyendo por la selva presurosos
se pierden de la noche los rumores;
los mochuelos ocúltanse medrosos
en las ruinas, y exhalan los alcores
sus primeros alientos deleitosos.
Abandona mis párpados el sueño,
la llanura despierta alborozada:
con su semblante pálido y risueño
la vino a despertar la madrugada.
Del Oriente los blancos resplandores
a aparecer comienzan; la cañada
suspira vagamente, el sauce llora
cabe la fresca orilla del riachuelo,
y la alondra gentil levanta al cielo
un preludio del himno de la aurora.
La bandada de pájaros canora
sus trinos une al murmurar del río;
gime el follaje temblador, colora
la luz el monte, las campiñas dora,
y a lo lejos blanquea el caserío.
Y va creciendo el resplandor y crece
el concierto a la vez. Ya los rumores
y los rayos de luz hinchen el viento,
hacen temblar el éter, y parece
que en explosión de notas y colores
va a inundar a la tierra el firmamento.

II

   Fleeing through the forest, the hurried
noises of the night are lost;
the little owls take shelter, fearful,
among the ruins, the hills exhale
their first delightful vapors.
Sleep abandons my eyelids,
the plain awakens to dawn's light:
The early morning, with its smiling and
pallid face, came to rouse the plain.
A white gleaming begins to appear
in the east; the stream makes what
sounds vaguely like a sigh, the willow
weeps on the cool banks of the little river,
and the noble lark lifts toward heaven
a prelude to the hymn of dawn.
The flock of song birds adds its warbles
to the murmur from the river; trembling
foliage moans, light floods the mountain,
the landscape is golden, and the village
in the distance glows white. The gleam
continues growing and, simultaneously,
the concert grows too. Now sounds
and light-beams swell the wind,
making ether quake, and the firmament,
exploding with music and color,
appears to inundate the earth.

III

    Allá, tras las montañas orientales,
surge de pronto el sol, como una roja
llamarada de incendios colosales,
y sobre los abruptos peñascales
ríos de lava incandescente arroja.
Entonces, de los flancos de la sierra
bañada en luz, del robledal obscuro,
del espantoso acantilado muro
que el paso estrecho a la hondonada cierra;
de los profundos valles, de los lagos
azules y lejanos que se mecen
blandamente del aura a los halagos,
y de los matorrales que estremecen
los vientos, de las flores, de los nidos,
de todo lo que tiembla o lo que canta
una voz poderosa se levanta
de arpegios y sollozos y gemidos.

    Mugen los bueyes que a los pastos llevan
silbando los vaqueros, mansamente
y perezosos van, y los abrevan
en el remanso de la azul corriente.
Y mientras de las cabras el ganado
remonta, despuntando los gramales,
torpes en el andar, los recentales
se quejan blanda y amorosamente
con un tierno balido entrecortado.

III

  There, behind the eastern range,
the sun suddenly surges, like a red
flame from colossal forest fires,
casting rivers of incandescent lava
over the rough-hewn rocky slopes.
Then, from the flanks of the light-bathed
sierra, from the dark oak grove,
from the frightening face of the cliff,
which closes off the ravine's narrow pass;
from the deep valleys, from the lakes,
distant and blue, which rock softly
back and forth to the flattery of breeze,
and from the scrubland, battered
by winds, from the flowers, from the nests,
from everything that trembles and sings,
a powerful voice is raised
in arpeggios, and sobs, and moans.

  The oxen, led to pasture by whistling
ranch-hands, bellow; they move tamely
and are lazy, as the cowboys water them
in the still pool formed off the blue current.
And while the flock of goats chews over
the clumps of grass sprouting up,
awkward in their amble, the unweaned
kids complain mildly and lovingly with
a tender, intermittent bleating. Down

Abajo, entre malla de raíces
que el tronco de las ceibas ha formado,
grita el *papán* y se oye en el sembrado
cuchichear a las tímidas perdices.
Mezcla aquí sus ruidos y sus sones
todo lo que voz tiene: la corteza
que hincha la savia ya, crepitaciones,
su rumor misterioso la maleza
y el *clarín de la selva* sus canciones.
Y a lo lejos, muy lejos, cuando el viento
que los maizales apacible orea
sopla del septentrión, se oye el acento
y algazara que, locas de contento,
forman las campanitas de la aldea . . .
¡Es que también se alegra y alboroza
el viejo campanario! La mañana
con húmedas caricias lo remoza;
sostiene con amor la cruz cristiana
sobre su humilde cúpula; su velo,
para cubrirlo, tienden las neblinas
como cendales que le presta el cielo
y, en torno de la cruz, las golondrinas
cantan, girando en caprichoso vuelo.

below, in the weave of roots formed
by the trunk of the ceiba trees,
the brown jay calls; and in the sown field
you can hear the rustling of timid quail.
Here the noises and sounds of everything
that has a voice mix: the tree's bark,
now swollen with sap, beginning to crack,
the undergrowth with its mysterious
murmurs and the thrush with its songs.
And in the distance, far away, when
the wind, which dries out fields of corn,
begins to blow from northern climes
you can hear the voice and uproar
that bells in the village contentedly toll . . .
Even the old bell tower takes heart
and is full of joy! The morning
renovates it with moist caresses;
the humble church dome holds
the Christian cross with love; and
the mists stretch their veil to cover it all
like fine silks on loan from heaven,
and the swallows sing, whirling round
and round the cross on whimsical wings.

IV

  Oigo pasar, bajo las frescas chacas,
que del sol templan los ardientes rayos,
en bandadas, los verdes guacamayos,
dispersas y en desorden las urracas.
Va creciendo el calor. Comienza el viento
las alas a plegar. Entre las frondas,
lanzando triste y gemidor acento,
la solitaria tórtola aletea.
Suspenden los sauces su lamento,
calla la voz de las cañadas hondas
y un vago y postrer hálito menea,
rozando apenas, las espigas blondas.

  Entonces otros múltiples rumores
como un enjambre llegan a mi oído:
el chupamirto vibra entre las flores;
sobre el gélido estanque adormecido
zumba el escarabajo de colores,
en tanto la libélula, que rasa
la clara superficie de las ondas,
desflora los cristales tembladores
con sus alas finísimas de gasa.

IV

Under the cool shade that tempers
the ardent rays of the sun, I hear
the green parrots passing in flocks,
scattered and disorderly like the magpies.
The heat is growing. The wind begins
to fold its wings. Among the fronds,
the solitary turtledove flutters and sends
forth her sad, whimpering tone.
The willows suspend their lament,
the voice of the deep ravines goes
silent, and a final, idle breeze
shakes, barely grazing, blond wheat.

Then other sounds, in multitudes
like a swarm, come to my ears:
the hummingbird vibrating among
the flowers; the colored beetle buzzing
over the cold, dormant pond, while
the dragonfly, skimming the clear
surface and its ripples, deflowers
the trembling crystal with
his finest wings of gauze.

El limpio manantial gorgoritea
bajo el peñasco gris que le sombrea,
corre sobre las guijas murmurando,
lame las piedras, los juncales baña
y en el lago se hunde; la espadaña
se estremece a la orilla susurrando
y la garza morena se pasea,
al son del agua cariñoso y blando.

The limpid wellspring warbles
beneath the gray boulder that shades it,
it runs murmuring over the pebbles, licks
the stones, bathes the reed bed and
then plunges into the lake; the cattail
shudders on the shoreline, whispering,
and the brown heron paces by
to water's rhythm, caring and mild.

V

Ya sus calientes hálitos la siesta
echa sobre los campos. Agostada
se duerme la amapola en floresta
y, muerta, la campánula morada
se desarraiga de la roca enhiesta;
pero en la honda selva estremecida
no deja aún de palpitar la vida:
toda rítmica voz la manifiesta.
No ha callado una nota ni un ruido:
en el espacio rojo y encendido
se oye a los cuervos crascitar, veloces
la atmósfera cruzando, y la montaña
devuelve el eco de sus roncas voces.
Las palomas zurean en el nido;
entre las hojas de la verde caña
se escucha el agudísimo zumbido
del insecto apresado por la araña;
las ramas secas quiébranse al ligero
salto de las ardillas, su chasquido
a unirse va con el golpeo bronco
del pintado y nervioso *carpintero*
que está en el árbol taladrando el tronco;
y las ondas armónicas desgarra,
con desacorde son, el chirriante
metálico estridor de la cigarra.

V

  The hour of siesta now throws its warm
breezes over the fields. The parched
poppy nods off in the forest, dead
roots of purple bellflower work free
and fall away from lofty rock;
but life's beating heart pulses yet
in the deep shuddering wood:
every rhythmic voice a witness.
Neither note nor noise fall silent:
the crows in the red hot midday air
can be heard cawing, swiftly crossing
the atmosphere, while mountain
returns echoes of their raspy calls.
The doves coo in their nests;
and among leaves of green reeds,
we hear the piercing buzz of insect
trapped in the spider's web;
the dry branches break under the weight,
even light, of squirrels' leap, the crack
joins in with the harsh hammering
of the colorful, if jumpy, carpenter bird,
whose beak drills deep in the tree's trunk;
and the harmonic waves are torn apart
by the discordant, creaking sounds
of the cicada's metallic chirp.

Corre por la hojarasca crepitante
la lagartija gris; zumba la mosca,
luciendo al aire el tornasol brillante
y, agitando su crótalo sonante,
bajo el breñal la víbora se enrosca.

  El intenso calor ha resecado
la savia de los árboles; cayendo
algunas hojas van y, al abrasado
aliento de la tierra evaporado,
se revienta la crústula crujiendo.
—En tanto yo, cabe la margen pura,
del bosque por los sones arrullado,
cedo al sueño embriagante que me enerva
y hallo reposo y plácida frescura
sobre la alfombra de tupida hierba.

The gray lizard skitters through a pile
of crunchy leaves; the fly buzzes by,
and the sunflower stands bright,
while the rattlesnake in the brush
shakes its tail and curls up tight.

  Intense heat has dried up the sap
from the trees; and burnt breeze
blowing over the evaporated land,
catches some leaves, while bark
on the trees crackles in the heat.
—I, meanwhile, on the edge
of the wood, lulled by forest sounds,
surrender to the intoxicating sleep
that weakens me, and I find
repose and placid cool on this
carpet of densely woven grass.

VI

  Trepando, audaz, por la empinada cuesta
y rompiendo los ásperos ramajes,
llego hasta el dorso de la abrupta cresta,
donde forman un himno a toda orquesta
los gritos de los pájaros salvajes.
Con los temblores del pinar sombrío
mezcla su canto el viento, la hondonada
su salmodia, su alegre carcajada
las cataratas del lejano río.
Brota la fuente en escondida gruta
con plácido rumor y, acompasada,
por la trémula brisa acariciada,
la selva agita su melena hirsuta.
Ésta es la calma de los bosques: mueve
blandamente la tarde silenciosa
la azul y blanca y ondulante y leve
gasa que encubre su mirar de diosa.

  Mas ya Aquilón sus furias apareja
y su pulmón la tempestad inflama.
Ronco alarido y angustiosa queja
por sus gargantas de granito deja
la montaña escapar; maldice, clama,
el bosque ruge y el torrente brama
y de las altas cimas despeñado,
por el espasmo trágico rompido,
rueda vertiginoso acantilado,

VI

  Boldly climbing up the steep slope
and breaking through the rough tangle
of branches, I reach the crest's sheer
edge where the calls of the wild birds
form their full, orchestral hymn.
To the quivering of the shadowy pine grove,
the wind adds its song, the hollow adds
its psalmody, and the distant river's
waterfall adds its joyful, hearty laughter.
With its placid sound, the spring rises up
from its hidden grotto and, keeping time,
the forest shakes its bristly mane,
caressed by the tremulous breeze.
This is the calm of the woods:
the quiet of the afternoon softly
concealing its goddess-like gaze in a
rolling, feather light gauze of blue and white.

  But soon the north wind prepares
its fury and fills its lungs with storm.
The mountain lets a hoarse scream
and anxious lament escape through
its granite throats; it curses and shouts;
the wood roars and the torrent growls,
an overhang falls from highest peaks,
and, broken by the tragic spasm,
rolls down the vertiginous cliff,

donde han hecho las águilas el nido
y su salvaje amor depositado;
y al mirarle por la tierra destruído,
expresión de su cólera sombría,
aterrador y lúgubre graznido
unen a la tremenda sinfonía.

   Bajo hasta la llanura. Hinchado el río
arrastra en pos peñascos y troncones
que con las ondas encrespadas luchan.
En las entrañas del abismo frío
que parecen hervir, palpitaciones
de una monstruosa víscera se escuchan.
Retorcidas raíces, al empuje
feroz, rompen su cárcel de terrones.
Se desgaja el espléndido follaje
del viejo tronco que al rajarse cruje;
el huracán golpea los peñones,
su última racha entre las grietas zumba
y es su postrer rugido de coraje
el trueno que, alejándose, retumba
sobre el desierto y lóbrego paisaje . . .

where the eagles have made their nest
and deposited all their savage love;
seeing the nest dashed to the earth,
they unite their terrifying, lugubrious
shrieks, a dark declaration of ire,
to the tremendous symphony.

  Dropping to the plain. The swollen river
drags, in its wake, boulders and large trunks
that struggle against the cresting waves.
In the bowels of the cold chasm,
which seem to boil, a monstrous and
visceral throbbing can be heard.
Twisted roots, straining under ferocious
pressure, break from their dirt clod jails.
The splendid foliage is snapped off
of the old trunk that creaks as it cracks;
the hurricane pounds the towering rocks,
its final gust whirls through crevices,
and its last courageous roar is thunder,
moving off in the distance, booming
over the deserted and gloomy landscape . . .

VII

  Augusta ya la noche se avecina
envuelta en sombras. El fragor lejano
del viento aun estremece la colina
y las espigas del trigal inclina,
que han dispersado por la tierra del grano.
Siento bajo mis pies trepidaciones
del peñascal; entre su quiebra obscura,
revuelto el manantial, ya no murmura,
salta, garrulador, a borbotones.
Son las últimas notas del concierto
de un día tropical. En el abierto
espacio del Poniente, un rayo de oro
vacila y tiembla. El valle está desierto
y se envuelve en cendales amarillos
que van palideciendo. —Ya el sonoro
acento de la noche se levanta.
Ya empiezan melancólicos los grillos
a preludiar en el solemne coro . . .
¡Ya es otra voz inmensa la que canta!

  Es el supremo instante. Los ruidos
y las quejas, los cantos y rumores
escapados del fondo de los nidos,
de las fuentes, los árboles, las flores;
el sonrosado idilio de la aurora,

VII

   Majestic now the night approaches,
enveloped in shadow. The distant roar
of the wind still trembles on the hill
and bends the wheat stalks on the field,
which have scattered their seed over the earth.
I feel the vibrations of the rocky slope
beneath my feet; in its dark breaks
the shaken spring no longer mumbles,
nor gushes forth in rolling boil as before.
These are the final notes of the concert
of a tropical day. In the open space
of the western horizon, a golden ray
vacillates and trembles. The valley is
deserted and wrapped in silken yellows
that fade to pale. Now the sonorous
accents of the night rise up. Now
crickets commence their melancholy
prelude in the solemn evening choir . . .
But already another immense voice sings!

   The moment is beyond compare. The noises
and complaints, the songs and sounds
escaped from the depths of nests,
from fountains, trees, and flowers;
the blushing idyll of dawn, which

de estrofas cremesinas que el sol dora,
la égloga de la verde pastoría,
la oda de oro que al mediar el día
de púrpura esplendente se colora,
de la tarde la pálida elegía
y la balada azul, la precursora
de la noche tristísima y sombría . . .
todo ese inmenso y continuado arpegio,
estrofas de una lira soberana
y versos de un divino florilegio,
cual bandada de pájaros canora
acude a guarecerse en la campana
de la rústica iglesia que, lejana,
se ve sobre las lomas descollando.
Y en el instante místico en que al cielo
el *Angelus* se eleva, condensando
todas las armonías de la tierra,
el himno de los bosques alza el vuelo
sobre lago, colinas, valle y sierra;
y, al par de la expresión que en su agonía
la tarde eleva a la divina altura,
del universo el corazón murmura
esta inmensa oración: ¡*Salve, María*!

the sun warms with crimson strophes,
the eclogue of verdant pasture,
the ode of gold, which puts on bright
purple robes when day intercedes,
the pallid elegy of the afternoon
and the blue ballad, precursor of
saddest and shadowy night . . .
all that immense and continuous
arpeggio, stanzas of a sovereign lyre
and verses of a divine anthology, like
a mellifluous flock of birds, comes
to take shelter in the bell tower
of a country church, standing out
over the hills in the distance.
And in that mystic instant in which
the *Angelus* rises to heaven, all
the harmonies of earth condensed,
the hymn of the woods takes flight
over lake and hill, over valley and peak;
and, as the afternoon in its agony
lifts its voice to divine heights,
the heart of the universe whispers
this cosmic invocation: *Salve, María!*

La montaña

El encinar solloza. La hondonada
que raja el monte es una boca ingente
por donde grita el bramador torrente
de furiosa melena desgreñada,

La piedra tiene acentos. Vibra cada
roca, como una cuerda, intensamente,
que en sus moles quedó perpetuamente
del Génesis la voz petrificada.

Del hondo seno de granito escucha
las voces, ¡oh poeta! Clama el oro:
¡Viva y goza, mortal! El hierro: *¡Lucha!*

Mas oye, al par, sobre la altura inmensa,
cantar en almo y perdurable coro
a las agudas cumbres: *¡Ora y piensa!*

Mountain

The oak grove weeps. The hollow
that cracks the mount is a vast mouth
through which the roaring torrent shouts,
a furious and disheveled flow.

The stone begins to speak. Each rock
vibrating intensely like a chord
that has waited forever in this block,
since Genesis, a petrified word.

Listen to the voices from this granite
bosom, Poet! The gold proclaims:
"Live, mortal, and enjoy!" While iron

shouts "Fight on!" But also hear on high,
enduring and divine, the sharpest peaks
in their choral song: "Pray and think!"

Pastoral

I

  Allá, sobre escarpada serranía,
enhiesto y colosal se empina un risco:
a su pie, retorciéndose bravía,
baja, por entre el roble y el lentisco,
una senda hasta humilde pastoría,
donde hay una cabaña y un aprisco.
Es solo habitador de aquel albergue,
un pobre rabadán: mas nunca el día
lo encontró bajo el rústico techado,
pues apenas ha el alba despuntado,
sus perlas derramando en cielo y tierra,
ya la figura del pastor se yergue
sobre el excelso pico de la sierra.
Como un dios se le mira desde el valle
en la roca granítica tallado,
majestuoso y altivo, acariciado
del trémulo pinar por el ventalle.
Y cuando el sol, al asomar, colora
de rosicler aristas y perfiles
y chorrea en los húmedos cantiles
el diluvio de rosas de la aurora,
las cabras y corderos triscadores
empiezan a saltar por los alcores,
que empenachan el mirto y la retama
y el heno alfombra y la menuda grama.

I

   There—over the soaring range
—a crag rises colossal and erect,
while at its foot a wild path twists
down through oak and mastic trees
toward the humble pasture where
there is a herder's hut and fold.
A poor shepherd is the sole inhabitant
of the abode, though daylight
never finds him beneath that rustic roof.
Day barely begins to break, its pearls
spilling out over heaven and earth,
when his figure stands out
over the high peak of that sierra.
Atop that granite perch and seen
from the valley below he seems
so like a god: chiseled, majestic, exalted,
caressed by breeze from trembling pines.
And when the sun, about to rise, paints
silhouette and ridge a rosy shade
pouring out onto dew-damp cliffs
a flood of roses, courtesy of dawn,
then goats and playful lambs begin
to bustle about the hills, adorned
by myrtle and broom shrub, along
with a carpet of hay and tufts of grass.

Se les ve, desde el fondo del paisaje,
sobre el musgoso peñascal salvaje
brillar al sol, blanquísimos y tersos,
como nevados ópalos, dispersos
entre las esmeraldas del frondaje.

Out of the backdrop of this landscape
the flock emerges so white and smooth
against the rocky wild moss-covered slope,
fleece shining in the sun like a powdery snow,
like opals scattered on leafy emerald canvas.

II

  Sumérgese el pastor, vagando libre
ya en las resplandecencias de la cima
o ya en las lobregueces del barranco,
sin que una sola víscera le vibre,
ni al resbalar por la espantosa sima,
ni al descender por la cortante flanco.
Es el rey y señor de la comarca
solamente habitada por las fieras
y las reses salvajes. Sus dominios,
do jamás hubo guerras ni exterminios,
del ingente peñón, erguido encima,
con sólo un golpe de su vista abarca.
Vertientes quebradísimas, laderas
en que se junta y amalgama el verde
con el violeta azul, y al fin se pierde,
al esfumarse en las lejanas eras;
dorsos de piedra rígidos que enarca
la montaña en tremendas convulsiones,
al sentir el furor de los turbiones;
parapetos de roca amenazando
aplastar los ramajes y los troncos;
guijas que arrancan de su lecho blando
los torrentes horrísonos y roncos
que al valle ruedan con fragor bramando;

II

  Roaming free, the shepherd is overtaken
by the brilliant glow, at times on the peak,
at others by the dark shadows of the ravine
yet nothing shakes his nerve,
not slipping along frightful chasm
nor descending steepest slopes, he is king,
the master of this realm of wild bulls
and other beasts. Standing atop
the enormous crag, with sweeping view,
he surveys the whole of his domain,
which has never witnessed war
or devastation: broken escarpments
and cliff faces on which green
and violet-blue amalgamate,
fusing fast only to fade away,
vanishing on the distant plains;
a rigid stone backbone arches over
the mountain with tremendous spasms
when it feels the fury of the storm,
rocky parapets threatening to crush
branches and trunks; vetch
uprooted from its soft bed
by the roaring, rushing torrent rolling
down the valley with a howling noise;

cavernas pavorosas, hondonadas
en donde se detienen las miradas
fijas, con estupor horrorizante,
del tenebroso piélago delante;
cumbres que irisa eternamente el hielo
y besan las purpúreas alboradas
y agujas de granito, donde el vuelo
las águilas abaten fatigadas
al terminar su viaje por el cielo . . .

terrifying caverns, dark hollows
where we fix our gaze
horrified yet amazed
in the face of that shadowy deep;
eternal ice of iridescent peaks
kissed by purple-colored dawns,
and granite spears where eagles beat
their exhausted wings, having
completed their journey through the sky . . .

III

   Abajo, la llanura, las vecinas
selvas; muy lejos, la ignorada aldea,
en el centro de un valle que rodea
el verde cinturón de las colinas;
cerca, los frescos y olorosos prados
en las estribaciones blandamente
de la agreste montaña recostados;
arriba, un océano: el oleaje
de las cimas riscosas y onduladas
que corren descendiendo gradualmente,
ya dóciles y tersas, ya encrespadas,
como olas en un mar que derrepente
cuajara el Septentrión; y en el encaje
de las tajadas peñas, el roquero
risco, cual torreón del homenaje
de un castillo fantástico y severo;
y en el último término, al escaso
resplandor de la tarde, las llanadas
silenciosas y tristes, y empapadas
en las cárdenas tintas del ocaso ...
tal es el reino del pastor.

III

  Below, the plain and neighboring
forests; far off, the forgotten village,
in the middle of a valley surrounded
by green belt of hills; close at hand,
the meadows, aromatic and cool,
reclining softly on the foothills
of that rugged mountain; and above,
an ocean: the tide of craggy and
undulating peaks running, falling
gradually, sometimes docile and smooth
but at others rough like the waves
in a sea whipped up of a sudden
by the old north wind; and in the lace
of sharpened crags, the rocky peak,
like an imposing tower of tribute
in some castle, fantastic and severe;
and at the end of the day, in scant glow
of evening light, there stand the plains,
muted and sad, and soaked
in the sunset's crimson hues . . .
Such is the shepherd's realm.

IV

                Impera
majestad absoluta y verdadera,
sobre aquella región, casi perdida
y extraña de los hombres a la vida;
pero donde otra vida omnipotente
del seno augusto de la tierra brota,
como alma inmensa por el aire flota,
y do la madre universal se siente
rayo en el éter y en las auras nota.
Bajo aquel dilatado firmamento,
nada el poder vivificante turba,
ni suspende el eterno movimiento.
Desde el hondo nivel de la planicie,
igual y recta, hasta la excelsa curva
trazada en la cerúlea superficie,
todo es fuerza y calor, todo es aliento.
La tierra ardiente se desborda en olas
de resonantes hierbas y corolas
y, cuando empieza a modular el viento
los himnos de su agreste sinfonía,
circula de la sierra por la espalda
un divino temblor. La selva umbría
que festonea la sinuosa falda,
esponja muellemente su ropaje
de pomposo y verdísimo follaje
como una ala de trémula esmeralda;

IV

                        He reigns
with a majesty absolute and true
over that region almost forgotten
and so strange to the life of men,
but where another, omnipotent life
sprouts from earth's august bosom like
an immense soul floating through the air,
where our universal mother is sensed
as a bolt in ether and note on the wind.
Beneath the expanding firmament
nothing clouds life-giving power,
nothing stays eternal movement.
From the lowest level of the plain,
even and straight, to the highest curve
traced in the cerulean spheres,
all is strength and warmth, all is breath.
The burning land overflows in waves
of resounding herbs and flower buds
and, when the wind begins to play
the hymns of its rugged symphony,
a divine tremor courses through
the sierra's spine. The shady forest
that festoons the sierra's sinuous skirt
absorbs with ease its garment
of pompous, greenest foliage
like a wing of shimmering emerald;

y, so las frondas vírgenes, el grano
y la yema y el óvulo que duermen,
se despiertan al soplo soberano
¡y todo vibra en la explosión del germen!
Nada yace en la calma y el reposo:
donde un átomo alienta hay un sonido,
un estremecimiento portentoso,
ya brisa, ya huracán, ¡siempre latido!
Al rodar, de las cumbres desprendido,
sobre los campos en fecundo riego,
el torrente, seméjase a un coloso
que se despeña desatado y ciego;
y, mientras el espacio enrojecido
arde como una bóveda de fuego,
y reverbera el sol en las opacas
moles de piedra, por el bosque añoso
aun se siente pasar el poderoso
aliento de las ondas genesiacas.

while beneath the virgin fronds,
sleepy grain and bud and ovule
awaken to the sovereign gust of air
and everything hums in the exploding seed!
Nothing lies in calm and repose:
where a single atom breathes, noise
abides, a portentous tremble, a breeze
at times, or hurricane, always heartbeat!
Rolling, unleashed from the heights,
over the fields in fertile spray,
the torrent seems a colossus
tumbling down, unhinged and blind;
and while crimson-colored space
smolders like a vault of fire,
and the sun reverberates on the opaque
mass of stone, the bracing breath
of the waves from Genesis may even
be felt passing through the age-old wood.

V

   Entonces, bajo el oro que el verano
difunde, como polen infinito,
a cuya influencia se madura el grano,
amarillea el césped en el llano
y el musgo se reseca en el granito,
el pastor, con alma estremecida,
responde, una por una, a las potentes
y raudas pulsaciones de la vida;
el sol canicular su sangre abrasa
que, por las anchas venas, a torrentes
con ritmo libre y vigoroso pasa;
y del espacio en la candente lumbre
clavando la mirada, y en los rojos
paisajes, por las siestas abrasados,
que surgen a lo lejos, tras la cumbre
de la montaña azul—inmensos prados
de secas yerbazales y rastrojos—
siente cual un sacudimiento enorme
penetrar en su alma la grandeza
de aquella tropical naturaleza
y la salvaje majestad. Informe
va esfumándose el cuadro ante sus ojos
y, levantando entonces la cabeza,
para explorar los vastos panoramas
del monte y la profunda lejanía,
trepa de un viejo tronco por las ramas,
y en la ardiente explosión del medio día
lo cubre el sol con su dosel de llamas.

V

   Then, beneath the gold bestowed
by Summer, like an infinite pollen,
under whose influence the grain grows
and the grasses of the plain yellow
and moss on the granite dries out,
the shepherd, with his soul astir,
responds to the swift and potent
pulsations of life—one by one;
the Dog Day sun inflames the blood
which throbs through his veins, flood
with a rhythm free and full of vigor;
and fixing his gaze on the bright lamp
of space, and on reddish landscapes
scorched by the middle hours of the day,
which rise in the distance behind the peak
of the blue mountain—immense fields
with dry stands of wild grass and weed—
he feels a sudden quake well up
within his soul as he beholds
the grandiosity of that tropical scene
and its savage majesty. The formless
painting evaporates before his eyes
and lifting his head then to explore
the sweeping panoramas of his
solitary mount and its vast remoteness,
he climbs into the branches of an old tree
and in the burning explosion of midday
the sun covers him with a canopy of flame.

VI

  Todo parece reposar en torno
al estival influjo del bochorno:
desde la base y áspera pendiente,
hasta la cumbre, donde apenas pudo
llegar la planta humana. En indolente
actitud yace el bruto. Desmayado
el sonoro follaje cuelga mudo,
cual harpa a sestear, blanco y lanudo,
bajo la sombra, el triscador ganado.
Sólo en las hondonadas más abruptas,
donde las fuentes gárrulas borbollan
y, dulcemente susurrando, arrollan
blandos líquenes y ovas incorruptas,
el recio leñador, casi desnudo,
hiende los troncos jadeando. El eco
a los golpes retumba, ya apagado
por la distancia, ya vibrante y hueco.
Y parece temblar la cordillera
y estremecerse el soto y la campaña,
como si a cada hachazo se sintiera
latir el corazón de la montaña.

VI

   All appears to be at rest under
the influence of sultry summer heat,
from mountain base and harsh slope
to the very peak, where human foot
could hardly tread. The beast lies
in indolent attitude. The once tuneful
foliage hangs withered and mute
like a sleepy harp, while the woolly
white lambs rest in the shade.
Only in the steepest ravines,
where the noisy springs bubble up
and, sweetly whispering, roll over
soft lichens and unspoiled algae,
the sturdy woodcutter, almost nude,
panting splits tree trunks. The echo
of the blows reverberates, muted
now by distance, hollow but resonant.
And mountain range seems to tremble,
and grove and field seem to quake,
as if we could feel with each axe-fall
the beating heart of the mountain.

VII

En las tardes azules, cuando otoña,
el pastor se recuesta sobre el césped
en lo más alto de la sierra, donde,
tañendo su tristísima zampoña,
oye que la torcaz, eterno huésped
del robledal, a su canción responde.
Y en las de invierno, diáfanas y frías,
cuando el rayo postrero resplandece,
ante las azuladas lejanías
abismado y absorto permanece.
Allá, cual vaga niebla, la profunda
masa de otras extensas serranías
ven sus ojos de águila. Más lejos,
semejando un celaje que se inunda
del crepúsculo gris en los reflejos,
una línea sutil, visible apenas:
¡la ancha faja del mar! Hacia otro lado
de un valle en el confín, las rancherías
dispersas entre páramo y sembrado,
frescos lagos y tórridas arenas;
y en el extremo, aun por el sol bañado,
donde van a morir las dos cadenas
de montañas, confuso y esfumado,
cual un manchón opaco y ceniciento,
ve el triste solitario de los montes
—a mirar lo infinito acostumbrado
y a esparcirse en los vastos horizontes—

VII

  In the clear-blue afternoons of autumn
the shepherd reclines on the grasses
in the highest reaches of the sierra
where he plays his saddest panpipes
and hears the wild pigeon, eternal guest
of oak groves, responding to his song.
And in winter afternoons, diaphanous and cold,
when the last ray of sun is shining out,
he remains engrossed and absorbed
by the bluish distance spread before.
There, like a hazy fog below, his eagle
eyes perceive the vastness of other ranges
extending toward the horizon. And beyond,
simulating a cloudscape flooded
by gray twilight's reflected light,
barely visible, a subtle line: the wide
sash of the sea! Toward the other side
of a valley on the horizon, stock farms
scattered among plateaus and plantings,
cool lakes and scorching sands;
and even farther away, still bathed by the sun,
where the two mountain chains
go to die, the sad solitary man of the mount
sees—accustomed as he is to stare
into the infinite and lose himself in that
vast panorama—blurry and confused,
like an opaque and ashen stain on his view,

el ruin y miserable hacinamiento
que forma la ciudad: ¡tapias y muros
y palacios y templos y obeliscos
que anonada, en los tiempos oscuros,
la triunfante grandeza de los riscos!
Y divisa el pastor, con la mirada
que hiende, poderosa, los espacios,
las torres muy pequeñas, los palacios
aun más pequeños ... ¿y los hombres? ... ¡Nada!
Y, buscando a sus ansias más anchura,
alza los ojos. —Ya del sol fulgura
solo un rayo glorioso, en el instante
que se hunde en Ocaso agonizante.
Lo azul, lo inmensamente azul, se pierde
en la infinita lontananza verde:
tiembla la luz, se funden los colores
en la comba del éter; un residuo
de la lumbre del sol con resplandores
flavos enciende el horizonte occiduo.
Y de pie, sobre el risco que es su trono,
ve el soberano, en místico abandono,
en sus dominios acabarse el día
y la noche empezar, vaga y sombría.
¡Hora augusta y sagrada! —El sol esparce
su oro ya muerto en los flotantes velos
que a ras del cerco horizontal condensa,
para encajar en él, como un engarce,
la divina turquesa de los cielos
y de los campos la esmeralda inmensa.

the wretched and miserable crowding
that is the city: barriers and walls
and palaces and temples and obelisks,
all of it overwhelmed in the shade cast
by the triumphant enormity of the crags!
And the shepherd makes out, with his
powerful stare, penetrating space,
the towers so tiny and the palaces
smaller still . . . and the humans? Nothing!
And anxious to find a more open stretch
he lifts his gaze. —Now a single, glorious
ray of sun blazes, only an instant, before
plunging into its agonizing twilight.
Blueness, the immense azure is lost
in the infinite green distance:
the light trembles, the colors fuse
in the ether's curvature; a residue
of the sun's glow with copper-colored
splendor lights up the western sky.
Standing on the crag that is his throne,
the sovereign, in mystical rapture, sees
day in his dominions fade away
and night begin, somber and uneasy.
Holy and exalted hour! —The sun scatters
its gold (fading in the floating veils,
condensing near the lower horizon)
to encompass, like a setting for a gem,
that divine turquoise of the heavens
and immense emerald of the fields.

VIII

  Deja entonces su trono de granito
y baja por la senda silencioso
y en honda paz. La noche y lo infinito
le hablan en derredor; mas no al reposo
lo invitan, que su alma aun se halla abierta
a ese clamor profundo y misterioso
de las cosas brotado, como un grito
del Universo; grito prepotente
que a una vida sublime nos despierta
y pone al corazón de Dios enfrente.
Para aquel olvidado sin amores,
a quien sólo natura da sus flores,
la noche es una madre: inmensamente
lo acaricia y acógelo en su seno,
siempre de sombra y de ternura lleno.
Sopla el aura a su oído mansamente,
suspirando canciones y querellas
y, cuando para orar alza la frente,
clavan en su pupila transparente
sus dardos de diamante las estrellas;
y lo inunda en su etérea catarata,
las noches diafanísimas de junio,
el tenue polvo azul, azul y plata,
en que envuelve a la tierra el plenilunio:
o bien, cuando en los montes se desata,
desde el alto crestón hasta el ribazo,
el viento bramador y enfurecido,
la noche para él tiene un latido

VIII

He leaves then his granite throne
and silently, in a deep calm, descends
along the trail. The night and infinity
speak all around him, but do not invite
him to repose, for his soul is still open
to that voice, mysterious and profound,
blossoming out of things, like a shout
from the Universe; a haughty shout that
awakens us to a life more sublime
and sets the heart of God before us.
For that loveless, forgotten one,
to whom only nature gives her flowers,
night is a caring mother: so immense
are her caresses, she draws him
to her bosom, always so full of tenderness
and shadow. The breeze blows softly
in his ear, whispering songs and complaints
and, when he lifts his brow to pray,
the stars fix their diamond darts
in the transparent pupils of his eyes;
and, in those clearest nights of June,
he is flooded by an ethereal cataract,
the tenuous azure dust, silver and blue,
in which Earth is wrapped by full moon:
even when the furious, bellowing wind
comes rushing through the mountains
from high crest down steep slopes,
the night cradles him in its lap

y un arrullo de amor, en su regazo.
¡Noches de santo horror e indefinible
misterio: ya reinéis claras u obscuras
mira el alma en vosotras lo invisible,
para sentir después, hondo y terrible,
el vértigo de Dios en las alturas!

with a heartbeat and a loving lullaby.
Nights of holy terror, mysteries
undefined: whether you rule with dark or light,
the soul sees in you everything invisible
in order to feel, later, deep and terrible,
the vertigo of God in soaring heights.

IX

Hay, en las soledades estrelladas
de aquellas noches, una inmensa y triste
serenidad. Cuando la luna llena
baña la sierra en ondas plateadas,
el pico enhiesto de esplendor se viste
y se incrusta en la atmósfera serena.
Como un diluvio la blancura llueve
y queda el aire convertido en ampo,
el agua en perlas y anegado el campo
en luminosos átomos de nieve.
Entonces más que nunca, desbordadas
las recónditas ansias que en el pecho
se agitan del pastor, siempre tranquilo
y humilde, pero nunca satisfecho,
al exterior asoman, condensadas
en profundas y límpidas miradas,
que se remontan hasta el almo asilo
de los mundos sin fin. Mientras reposa
el cuerpo laxo sobre el duro lecho
en la divina cúpula radiosa
—dejando lo finito de la tierra
y libre de los misérrimos pesares—
el levantado espíritu se encierra.
Sólo el cielo en las noches estelares,
cuando brillan los astros a millares
y a millares se agrupan, ocultando
el ancho velo de zafiro; cuando
forman islas sin playas en los mares

IX

In the starry solitude of those nights
there is a sad and immense calm.
When full moon bathes mountains
in silvery waves, the soaring peak
is clothed in splendor, embedded
in such a serene atmosphere.
All in a deluge, the whiteness rains down
and the air is blanched a hoary pale,
the water changed to pearl, the fields
flooded by motes as luminous as snow.
Then, more than ever, the hidden overflow
of a longing is stirred within the shepherd's
usually tranquil, humble, yet unsatisfied breast;
a hidden angst outwardly manifests,
condensed in the deep and limpid gaze,
climbing toward the holy sanctuary of
world upon world. While the body, lax,
reposes on its hard bed, the elated
spirit—leaving the finite earth behind,
freed then from its wretched troubles—
takes refuge in that dome of divine rays.
Only the sky in those stellar nights,
when the stars shine by the thousands
and in the thousands cluster, obscuring
the vast sapphire veil; when the shoreless
islands take shape on the eternal seas

eternos del espacio . . . ¡sólo el cielo
que es reposo inmortal de todo anhelo
con sus fulgores y tristezas calma
el anhelo ardentísimo de una alma
plena de inmensidad!

X

                La noche cae
y reinan las tinieblas pavorosas.
Hay vértigo en el alma de las cosas
porque el horror, como el abismo, atrae.
Mas el pastor descansa. Ningún peso
viene a oprimir su corazón de justo;
ningún vestigio en su semblante impreso
ha dejado el dolor. Silencio augusto
impera en torno de él y, mientras duerme,
su perro en vela está, y el mal, inerme.
Repose en calma. La diurnal tarea
ya pronto volverá, pues tras el monte
una indecisa claridad blanquea . . .
Ya en las cumbres destácase el granito.
Ya se bañan de azul el horizonte
y el alma . . . .
                ¡Oh, infinito! ¡Oh, infinito!

of space . . . Only the night sky,
which is immortal repose of all desire,
with its resplendence and sorrow,
can calm the most ardent longing
of a soul full of immensity!

X

                      Night falls
and the frightful shadows reign over all.
A vertigo hovers above the world's soul
because horror attracts like the abyss.
But the shepherd rests. No weight
comes to oppress his upright heart;
grief has left no vestige stamped upon
his countenance. An august silence
prevails around him and, while he sleeps,
his dog keeps vigil and evil is held at bay.
Let him rest in calm. The diurnal labors
will soon return, for behind the mountain
a hesitant light whitens the sky again . . .
And already on the peaks the granite bulks
against that horizon bathed in blue
and the soul . . .
        Oh, infinity! Oh, infinite one!

En el desierto. Idilio salvaje/
In the Desert. Wild Idyll

I

¿Por qué a mi helada soledad viniste
cubierta con el último celaje
de un crepúsculo gris? . . . Mira el paisaje,
árido y triste, inmensamente triste.

Si vienes del dolor y en él nutriste
tu corazón, bien vengas al salvaje
desierto, donde apenas un miraje
de lo que fue mi juventud existe.

Mas si acaso no vienes de tan lejos
y en tu alma aun del placer quedan dejos,
puedes tornar a tu revuelto mundo.

Si no, ven a lavar tu cyprio manto
en el mar amarguísimo y profundo
de un triste amor, o de un inmenso llanto.

I

    Why have you come to my frozen solitude
covered in the gray twilight of this final
cloudscape? . . . Gaze upon the landscape
arid and sad, so immensely sad.

    If you come from the land of grief,
nourishing your heart on pain . . . you are
welcome in this barren place, where not
even a mirage of my lost youth remains.

    But if you don't come from that far away
and traces of pleasure still linger in your soul . . .
well, you can go back to your bustling world.

    If not, come wash your Cyprian mantle
in this bitter deep sea of sad love
or in this immensity of mourning.

II

  Mira el paisaje: inmensidad abajo,
inmensidad, inmensidad arriba:
en el hondo perfil, la sierra altiva
al pie minado por horrendo tajo.

  Bloques gigantes que arrancó de cuajo
el terremoto, de la roca viva;
y en aquella sabana pensativa
y adusta, ni una senda, ni un atajo.

  Asoladora atmósfera candente,
do se incrustan las águilas serenas
como clavos que se hunden lentamente.

  Silencio, lobreguez, pavor tremendos
que viene sólo a interrumpir apenas
el galope triunfal de los berrendos.

II

Look upon the landscape: immensity
below, immensity, immensity above:
in deep silhouette, the haughty sierra
mined at its base by horrendous gash.

Gigantic blocks, ripped from the heart
of living rock by an earthquake; and
in that contemplative, sober savannah
not a single trail or road in sight.

A devastating atmosphere, candescence
in which serene eagles stake claim
like railroad spikes slowly sinking in.

Silence, gloom, tremendous terror
punctuated only—and barely even then
—by the pronghorns' triumphal dash.

III

En la estepa maldita, bajo el peso
de sibilante brisa que asesina,
yergues tu talla escultural y fina
como un relieve en el confín impreso.

El viento entre los médanos opreso,
canta como una música divina,
y finge, bajo la húmeda neblina,
un infinito y solitario beso.

Vibran en el crepúsculo tus ojos,
un dardo negro de pasión y enojos
que en mi carne y mi espíritu se clava;

y destacada contra el sol muriente,
como un airón, flotando inmensamente,
tu bruna cabellera de india brava.

III

  On the ill-starred steppe, under the weight
of a whistling, murderous breeze,
your figure, sculpted and fine, is pressed
onto the horizon like a bass relief.

  The wind among the sand dunes sings
beneath the morning's humid mist,
as if its music were something divine,
feigning an infinite and solitary kiss.

  Your eyes shimmer in the twilight,
a black dart of fury and passion
piercing my flesh and my spirit;

  and standing out against the dying sun,
floating in the air like a royal heron:
your black hair of fierce Indian maiden.

IV

La llanada amarguísima y salobre,
enjuta cuenca de océano muerto
y, en la gris lontananza, como puerto,
el peñascal, desamparado y pobre.

Unta la tarde en mi semblante yerto
aterradora lobreguez, y sobre
tu piel, tostada por el sol, el cobre
y el sepia de las rocas del desierto.

Y el regazo donde sombra eterna,
del peñascal bajo la enorme arruga,
es para nuestro amor nido y caverna,

las lianas de tu cuerpo retorcidas
en el torso viril que te subyuga,
con una gran palpitación de vidas.

IV

This salty and most bitter plain,
dry basin of a dead ocean, and
in the gray distance, like a port:
rock formation—wretched, exposed.

Afternoon anoints my stiffening face
with dreadful gloom, while over your
complexion, bronzed by the sun, copper
and sepia tones from desert stone.

And in the lap of eternal shade
under the rocky outcrop's overhang—
a sheltering cave for our love—

your body's liana vines twist round
the virile trunk that holds you bound,
two palpitating lives entwined.

V

¡Qué enferma y dolorida lontananza!
¡qué inexorable y hosca la llanura!
flota en todo el paisaje tal pavura
como si fuera un campo de matanza.

Y la sombra que avanza . . . avanza, avanza,
parece, con su trágica envoltura,
el alma ingente, plena de amargura,
de los que han de morir sin esperanza.

Y allí estamos nosotros, oprimidos
por la angustia de todas las pasiones,
bajo el peso de todos los olvidos.

En un cielo de plomo el sol ya muerto;
y en nuestros desgarrados corazones
¡el desierto, el desierto . . y el desierto!

V

   How sickly and afflicted this open space,
this plain, so sullen and inexorable!
Such a fear floats over the landscape
as if it were a stock-yard slaughtering floor.

   And the shadow advancing . . . advancing
with its tragic wrapping . . . seems full
of bitterness, the enormous soul
of those who must die without hope.

   And there we are, overwhelmed
by the anxiety of every passion,
under the weight of all that's forgotten.

The sun now dead in this lead-gray sky
and in the open wound of our hearts:
desert, desert . . . and more desert.

VI

¡Es mi adiós! . . . Allá vas, bruna y austera,
por las planicies que el bochorno escalda,
al verberar tu ardiente cabellera
como una maldición sobre tu espalda.

En mis desolaciones, ¿qué me espera?
—ya apenas veo tu arrastrante falda—
una deshojazón de primavera
y una eterna nostalgia de esmeralda.

El terremoto humano ha destruído
mi corazón y todo en él expira.
¡Mal hayan el recuerdo y el olvido!

Aun te columbro y ya olvidé tu frente:
sólo, ¡ay!, tu espalda miro, cual se mira
lo que huye y se aleja eternamente.

VI

It's my goodbye! ... There you are, dark
and austere, moving over oven-scorched
plains, your ardent hair flowing
like an evil spell down your back.

In my desolation… what is left for me?
I barely see the flutter of your skirt now—
an explosion of leaves in spring
and eternal nostalgia for emerald green.

A human earthquake has demolished
my heart, everything inside it expires.
A curse on memory and the forgotten!

I can just barely make you out, though I've
forgotten your face, I see only your back
which looks forever like an escape.

VII

Envío

  En tus aras quemé mi último incienso
y deshojé mis postrimeras rosas.
Do se alzaban los templos de mis diosas
ya sólo queda el arenal inmenso.

  Quise entrar en tu alma, y ¡qué descenso!
¡qué andar por entre ruinas y entre fosas!
¡A fuerza de pensar en tales cosas
me duele el pensamiento cuando pienso!

  ¡Pasó!. . . ¿Qué resta ya de tanto y tanto
deliquio? En ti no la moral dolencia,
ni el dejo impuro, ni el sabor del llanto.

  Y en mí, ¡qué hondo y tremendo cataclismo!
¡qué sombra y qué pavor en la conciencia
y qué horrible disgusto de mí mismo!

VII

Envoi

  I burned my last incense on your altars
and scattered the petals of my final roses.
Where temples to my goddesses once
were erected, now only unending sand.

  I tried entering your soul . . . what a descent!
Such a journey among ruins, among
graves! When I am forced to think
about such things, it pains me even more!

  It happened! . . . Now what remains
of so much ecstasy? For you, not a twinge
of guilt, no impure trace, nor hint of weeping.

  And in me . . . profound, tremendous cataclysm,
such a dreadful shadow hovering over
my conscience, such terrible self-loathing.

NOTES

Prologue

1. In editing the poems of Othón for this collection, I have had constantly at hand the first edition of *Poemas rústicos* (México, 1902), from which most of the poems have been selected, along with another early edition of his selected poetry, published posthumously in the Cultura series by Loera y Chávez (México, 1917). Both early editions have been digitized and can be read through Internet Archive or the Biblioteca Virtual Miguel de Cervantes and their Biblioteca Virtual de Letras Mexicanas. The modern editions of Calvillo (1944), Castro Leal (1974), and especially Peñalosa (1997), have been helpful as well for consulting variants. Peñalosa, for example, traces all extant copies of the poems before their publication in *Poemas rústicos*, which is extremely useful for establishing chronology. Consulting Othón's poetry as collected in anthologies over the last century, has also been instrumental in getting a sense of changing tastes over the decades; see Paz (1985), Pacheco (1999), and Zaid (2003) for late-twentieth century examples.

2. Vicente Huidobro's poem *Arte poética*, originally published in his collection *El espejo de agua* (1916), has been anthologized many times over, see for example: Anderson Imbert and Florit 1970, 2: 258; Chang-Rodríguez and Filer 2004, pp. 341-42; Garganigo et al. 2002, p.423; Tapscott 1999, pp. 117-18. See also the biographical introduction of Fonseca 2010, pp. 66-69.

3. On nineteenth-century landscape, see Paz 1987 (quotations on p. 288); on landscape art in the trajectory of Mexican art history, see Smith 1968 and Fernández 1967; on José María Velasco in particular, see Ramírez 2017.

4. In addition to the notes on the poet to be found in the standard manuals, literary histories, and anthologies, my biographical sketch of Othón draws on the biography of Zavala 1952, the introductions and

notes of Castro Leal 1974 and Peñalosa 1997, and the monographic study of Montejano y Aguiñaga 1997.

5. On this characterization of nineteenth-century Mexican poetry see González Peña (1945, p. 269); but also the criticism of Paz 1985, pp. 31-32.

6. González Peña 1945, p. 279; 1949, pp. 312-13. The characterization of Othón as a "modern bucolic poet" is from Isaac Goldberg's note in Blackwell (1937, p. 538), but was a common misconception in the poet's own lifetime according to Zavala.

7. See Zavala 1952, pp. 41-42.

8. Peñalosa (1997, 1: 261-63) includes Othón's prologue in his edition: "Es necesario considerar en el Arte lo que es en sí: no sólo una cosa grave y seria, sino profundamente religiosa, porque el Arte es religión, en cuanto a Belleza y en cuanto a Verdad, y uno de los vínculos, acaso el más fuerte, que nos liga con la eterna Verdad y con la Belleza Infinita" (1: 261)

9. "...el Arte no puede, no debe ser tomado como pasatiempo, ocio o distracción, sino que hay que consagrar a él todas las energías del corazón, del cerebro y de la vida" (in Peñalosa 1997, 1: 262).

10. "La musa no ha de ser un espíritu extraño que venga del exterior a impresionarnos, sino que ha de brotar de nosotros mismos para que, al sentirla en nuestra presencia, en contacto con la Naturaleza, deslumbradora, enamorada y acariciante, podamos exclamar en el deliquio sagrado de la admiración y del éxtasis, lo que el padre del género humano ante su divina y eterna desposada: '*Os ex ossibus meis et caro de carne mea!*'" (in Peñalosa 1997, 1: 261).

11. I cite the letter as it appears in the facsimile edition of *Lascas* (Díaz Mirón 1984, p. VII-IX).

12. See Díaz Mirón (1984, p. 101): "El sitio es ingrato, por fétido y hosco. / El cardón, el nopal y la ortiga / prosperan; y el aire trasciende a bóñiga, / a marisco y a cieno; y el mosco / pulula y ostiga."

13. "Su naturaleza era la naturaleza americana, con rastros de catástrofes y derrumbes terciarios, donde pesadas moles de geometrías fantásticas esculpen un paisaje majestuoso y bronco, de admiración y espanto; donde el sol de cuatro siglos ha calcinado los desiertos reverberantes que rebajan la línea del horizonte; donde las aguas incontenibles, inmensas, arrolladoras, han horadado montes y sierras, dejando al correr, turbias de arena, su recuerdo en espeluncas, hondonadas y barrancos. Naturaleza de moles abruptas y majestuosas, de tupidas selvas tropicales, alumbrada por relámpagos y sonora de tormentas, turbiones y diluvios" (1974, p. XI).

14. On Bello and Heredia, see Chang-Rodríguez and Filer (2004, pp. 93-117), Anderson Imbert and Florit (1970, 1: 248-72), Garganigo et al (2002, pp. 197-205, 219-27).

15. See Benedetti (1992): "El paisaje textual de un Othón, la pincelada trémula de un Zorrilla de San Martín, o la versión sensual de Heredia, parecen hoy en día más lejanos que Homero" (pp. 361-62).

16. See Othón 1917, p. 6.

17. In his notes to Blackwell 1937, p. 538.

18. In the "History of Mexican Poetry" included as an introduction to *Mexican Poetry: An Anthology*, originally published in 1958 (Paz 1985, p. 32).

19. Pacheco (1999, p. 68): "toda su obra parece un ejercicio de estilo para escribir el 'Idilio salvaje'."

20. Castro Leal (1974, p. vii): "De todos los grandes poetas mexicanos Manuel José Othón es el menos leído y también el menos apreciado; en el extranjero apenas se conoce."

21. Othón's letter to Juan B. Delgado: "En los poetas sudamericanos todo es convencionalismo, rebuscamiento, prurito de ser únicos; no hay nada sincero, ni espontáneo, por más que haya muchas veces una labor primorosa" (qtd. in Díaz Mirón 1984, p. VIII). On Spanish-American

modernism, its evolving legacy in Latin American letters, and recent critical reappraisals, see Washbourne 2007, along with the introductions in Stavans 2011, Tapscott 1999, Pacheco 1999, and Gallagher 1974; on its influence in Mexico in particular, see Bell 1987, Álvarez 1971, González Peña 1945, 1949.

22. González Peña 1945, pp. 278-79.

23. This was from an article Urbina published in *El mundo ilustrado* (23 Jul 1905): "La poesía de Othón es una maravilla de verdad, de energía, de sentimiento de la vida. Su obra, que es de las que han vencido, será de las que perduran. Está pensada y sentida en la altura de ideal; está tallada en mármol" (qtd. in Montejano y Aguiñaga 1997, p. 177)

24. For the original Spanish version of the poem "Paisaje," see Huidobro 2010, p. 72; Torres-Ríoseco's critique of Huidorbro (1967, p. 124) includes a translation of this poem into English, as an example of *Creacionismo*'s inability to live up to its promises: "he [Huidobro] gave expression to poetical theories which attracted wide attention, but his creative work was not able to maintain his reputation. The reader may judge for himself why, from this sample poem."

25. "En el fondo, Velasco fue víctima de ese a todas luces cruel, pero insoslayable, relevo generacional que, entre muchas otras cosas, afecta los gustos artísticos" (Ramírez 2017, p. 103).

Surgite!

The title is Latin for "Arise!" Originally, this sequence was written in 1890 and published in the August 17 edition of *El Estandarte* of San Luis Potosí. Joaquín Antonio Peñalosa (1997, 1: 264-65) notes a manuscript version among the Othón papers in the Universidad Autónoma Potosina (UAP), dated August 13.

Voz interna / Inner Voice

Peñalosa (1997, 1: 269) tells us that there is a manuscript in the UAP dated May of 1889 (apparently written in Tula de Tamaulipas) and that the poem was published at various points with the title

"Íntima." It first appeared in 1895 in the famous modernist *Revista Azul*, though the theme is very much in keeping with the romantics (we could easily see this poem written by a brooding Baudelaire, for example).

Crepúsculos / Twilights

Also written in Tamaulipas in 1889 (February), according to Peñalosa (1997, 1: 271), this pair of sonnets—to sunrise and sunset twilights—has in common with some of his earliest poetry a tendency toward the mystical. The pair was published with the subtitle "En la sierra" (in the mountains) in the March 3 edition of *El Estandarte*.

Paisajes / Landscapes

The UAP has a couple of early manuscripts (both dated in 1889) of this pair of sonnets. The first manuscript is dedicated to Manuel Gutiérrez Nájera, Othón's contemporary, the more famous Mexican poet, whose work often appears in the anthologies of Latin American *Modernismo*. The sequence appears in print three times before *Poemas rústicos* between 1889 and 1899, including the February 17, 1895 issue of *Revista Azul*. Manuel Calvillo (1944, p. 173) notes that the first appearance in print in *Revista de Letras y Ciencias* (1889) was also dedicated to Gutiérrez Nájera.

Meridies is Latin for Midday; *Noctifer*, Latin for nightfall. In spite of the classical form (the sonnet) and the Latin titles (a modernist tendency, as for example in Gutiérrez Nájera's "Pax Anima" and "Non Omnis Moriar"), the tropical fauna is not typical of the escapist lyric of early modernism and anticipates their late turn toward a recognizably American landscape in, for example, the early twentieth-century poetry of Rubén Darío or José Santos Chocano. Zavala (1952, pp. 86-87) reports that Othón had been reading Pagaza's *Murmurios de la selva* intensely in 1887-1888, the only decent Mexican model for his work in this period.

Lobreguez / Gloom

This poem was written very much in the spirit of the Romantics and their obsession with twilights, gloomy ruins and graveyards. In Mexico the trend can be seen with poems like Justo Sierra's "Bucolic Funeral" or Manuel Acuña's "Before a Corpse," though both of these poems have their rays of hope. Hope appears absent from the Othonian landscape of "Gloom." Nonetheless, our poet manages to evoke a specifically Mexican landscape in a way that the "Bucolic" setting of Sierra's poem does not. The horse droppings and cow patties of the corral's sticky floor, baking in the sun for most of the day, add to the fetid *vaho* that hangs in the air. The abandoned convent, falling to ruins calls to mind the confiscations and reform laws of the Juárez years, and their impact on the landscape (for basic overview of the political context, see Fuentes, Arciniegas).

Peñalosa characterizes this poem as a "fragmento de una leyenda inédita" (fragment of an unpublished legend). It was initially titled "Scherzo trágico" and published in this fragmentary form in *El Estandarte* in 1895, the only other time it appears in print before the *Poemas rústicos* collection of 1902. The "fragments" reflect, in a way, the very subject matter of the poem: the gloomy remains of a small town in the waning twilight of its existence. Only the owls and coyotes are left to stalk the graveyard.

In the final stanza, Othón alludes to the "hyenas" and their their spasmodic howling. I have respected Othón's choice in the translation, even though there are no hyenas in the western hemisphere… well, literally speaking at least. I am certain he has in mind the coyotes, true American hyenas, whose spasmodic howls do indeed raise the hair on the back of your neck. I remember, for example, one evening outside a nursing home on the edge of McAllen in far south Texas: my wife was inside finishing up a visit with Granny Garza and I was in the parking lot watching our two young boys… all of a sudden, a pack of coyotes in the brush beyond the field across the road began making such a racket it sounded like a witches orgy, I expected flying monkeys to descend on us at any moment.

Ocaso / Sunset

Othón dedicates this poem "to a painter" and addresses the sonnet to him. In pointing out the landscape his interlocutor should paint, of course, our poet is in fact painting the scene for our imagination. Is he looking upon a real landscape or another artist's landscape painting? Another possibility: Othón may be having a bit of fun with the reader/painter, listing all the stock images of the landscape paintings of the day. The beauty of the written landscape is that it can call to mind a nearly infinite series of individual paintings.

The word "celaje" in the original Spanish is a common one at the time (Othón uses it several times in his oeuvre, as does Amado Nervo, who has a poem entitled "Celaje"). Where *paisaje* is a landscape, *celaje* can be a cloudscape (an important, though easily overlooked element in landscape paintings). The *Diccionario de la lengua española* (DLE) gives several definitions, the first of which is indeed quite painterly: "aspecto que presenta el cielo cuando ha nubes tenues y de varios matices" (aspect presented by the sky when it has thin clouds of various shades). I translate "cloud break" here instead of "cloudscape" only because I used the word "landscape" at the end of the first line.

Peñalosa dates this poem to 1894, though it does not appear in print before *Poemas rústicos* in 1902.

Nostálgica / Nostalgic

The epigraph is "Oh, where are the fields!" from Virgil's Georgics, Bk II. Peñalosa lists this poem among those of undated composition, though it would seem to be of a piece with "Gloom" (from 1895). In addition to the Virgilian inspiration, we can also point to the "Beatus ille" poems of Horace and Fray Luis de León: the longing to return to the country from the perspective of the hustle and bustle of the city. Othón adds to his classical and Renaissance sources the motif of the "coldness" of the city as opposed to the warmth of his home country (a tropical or sub-tropical warmth in this case). In keeping with the Romantic tendency for overdramatizing emotional states, Othón's nostalgia for the blue and green hues, and wide-open spaces of the mountains, soon gives way to a morbid fascination with the many ways he could die a sudden and gruesome death there, which is still preferable to the "losa sepulcral" (sepulchral slab or gravestone) weighing him down in the icy city.

Himno de los bosques / Hymn of the Woods

The *Angelus* is a call to prayer (often rung out from church bells) at dawn, noon, and sunset. *Salve, María* from the Ave María (Hail, Mary), which begins "Dios te salve, María"; the Ave María often concludes the *Angelus* prayers. Zavala (1952, pp. 86-99) has excellent notes on the evolution of this work, its precursors in Othón's own early work and its initial impact. Both Zavala and Peñalosa place the original composition in late 1890, early 1891, before its publication in *El Estandarte* and *El correo de San Luis* in April 1891. Zavala reports that Othón's reading and re-reading of Pagaza's 1887 collection encouraged the poet to dust off Virgil and Garcilaso (*Murmurios* contains Pagaza's translations of Virgil's eclogues in addition to his original poetry). These readings, in combination with his frequent excursions into the sierra, mark his definitive turn toward nature and landscape as the focus of his poetry.

La montaña / The Mountain

This sonnet is poem XVII of the "Noche rústica de Walpurgis" lyric sequence, the only one we include from that sequence in this collection, though these sonnets are among the most admired of his compositions (perhaps owing to their more Modernist aesthetic). Composed in 1897.

Pastoral

This long sequence appeared in print twice in 1899, in *El Estandarte* and the *Revista Moderna*; in an 1899 letter to Juan B. Delgado, Othón claims to have spent almost two years writing it (Peñalosa 1997, 1: 337). "Pastoral," along with other long poems such as the "Hymn of the Woods," has reinforced the notion of Othón as a "bucolic" poet, but it is interesting to compare the traditional descriptions of the "pastoral" mode with what it is that Othón actually depicts in his poetry. J. A. Cuddon (1992), in his "Pastoral" entry, writes "For the most part pastoral tends to be an idealization of shepherd life, and, by so being, creates an image of a peaceful and uncorrupted existence; a kind of pre-lapsarian world" (p. 686), or again later "Fundamentally, this is what pastoral is about: it displays a nostalgia for the past, for some hypothetical state of love and peace which has somehow been lost. The dominating idea and theme of most pastoral is the search for the simple life away from the court and town, away from corruption, war, strife, the love of gain, away from 'getting and spending'. In a way it reveals a yearning for a lost innocence, for a pre-Fall paradisal life in which man existed in harmony with nature" (p. 689). Cuddon then points out that in the eighteenth and nineteenth centuries poets tended to point out the rougher edges of rustic life with more realism (pp. 690-91), which is certainly the case with Othón and his insistence on storms, quakes, scalding heat, etc. (cf. "Pastoral" entry in Preminger et al 1974, pp. 603-606). Othón, if not a *positivista* or *científico* himself, has a much more "naturalistic" outlook in his poetry: man is diminutive in the landscape; but man is also a privileged spectator in the theater of wonder that is Nature.

In section VIII of the *Poemas rústicos* (1902) version of the text, we find one of the few typographical errors of the whole volume: *a quien sólo natura de [sic] sus flores*. It reads "...da sus flores" in other editions.

En el desierto. Idilio salvaje / In the Desert. Wild Idyll

This sonnet sequence is generally known as "Idilio salvaje" (or "Wild Idyll"), though it initially had the title "En el desierto" ("In the Desert"). As we mention above in the prologue, José Emilio Pacheco (1999, p. 68) has said of Othón that "toda su obra parece un ejercicio de estilo para escribir el 'Idilio salvaje'" [his entire body of work seems an exercise in style for writing "Wild Idyll"]. Octavio Paz (1985, p. 32) considered it the best of Othón's poetry as well, though this is perhaps more a reflection of their generation's aesthetic preferences (an earlier generation of critics, still under the thrall of *Modernismo*, preferred the sonnets in the "Noches rústicas de Walpurgis" sequence). "Wild Idyll" is certainly the most "modern" of Othón's lyrics, perhaps even anticipating certain avante garde tendencies: if much of Othón's work conforms in spirit to the great landscape painters of his day working in the realist or naturalist traditions, "Wild Idyll" seems more like a Georgia O'Keefe landscape. The play on landscape, angst and sexual tension, forbidden love, all suggest a return to late-Romantic themes, but Othón's treatment of them is extremely modern, and anticipates the César Vallejo of *Los heraldos negros* by more than a decade.

Sonnet I: See my note to the poem "Ocaso" (above) on the word *celaje*, which Samuel Beckett translates as "the dying rack." In this sonnet and the next, Beckett translates "Mira el paisaje" [Look at the landscape] as "Behold the scene."

Sonnet II: I interpret "berrendos" in the final verse as North American pronghorn antelopes, not uncommon in the northern deserts of Mexico (cf. definition #3 in the DLE's "berrendo" entry). Beckett translates this as "dappled deer."

Sonnet III: Peñalosa (1997, I: 508) has a note about "brisa" [breeze] in the poem's second line, which was erroneously printed as "grisa" when the sequence was first published in *El Mundo Ilustrado* (1906), a reading which Peñalosa keeps in his edition; we follow Calvillo, Zaid and others who have printed the line with "brisa." Beckett interprets the "airón" of the final tercet as a "crest of plumes," which would be consistent with indigenous headgear and is indeed one of the definitions of the word. Othón uses the word several times over the course of his poetic oeuvre (once to describe tufts of cotton in a field, for example, and again to describe the tongues of flame visible at the mouth of a volcano), so I have gone back and forth on this, but finally chosen to translate "airón" here as the royal heron ("garza real" is the DLE's first definition of "airón"), assuming that Othón had in mind the graceful flight of this majestic bird when "inmensamente flotando" on the air—not unlike the woman's black hair.

Sonnets IV-VI: The poet contrasts the barren, desert landscape (employing imagery that suggests death or approaching death, representing his age and failing health) with the green of springtime trying to find hospitable ground. The maiden's youth and beauty are, obviously, the green spring. The shade or shadow that might provide some respite from the scorching sun simultaneously conjures the tropical green vines and foreshadows the poet's demise.

Sonnet VII: The title, "Envío" is a reference to the poetic *envoi*, which Preminger et al. (1974, p. 242) describe as a "short concluding stanza found in certain Fr[ench] poetic forms"; often its "true function . . . was to serve as a pithy summing-up of the poem."

See Peñalosa's notes on "Wild Idyll" (1997, 1: 508) on dates of composition and variants. A letter to Juan B. Delgado dated to August of 1904 contains a transcription of all but sonnet VI and an introductory sonnet, which appears to attribute the sequence's mysterious love affair to artist Alfonso Toro. Many critics, however, assume that the lyric sequence reflects a late (and surprising) love interest of the poet himself. The poems were published only posthumously by *Revista Moderna* and *El Mundo Ilustrado* in December of 1906.

REFERENCES

Alegría (1974), Fernando. "Spanish American Poetry" in Preminger et al. 1974: 792-98.
Álvarez Z (1971), María Edmée. *Literatura mexicana e hispanoamericana: Manual para uso de las escuelas preparatorias.* México, DF: Editorial Porrúa.
Anderson-Imbert (1970), Enrique and Eugenio Florit. *Literatura hispanoamericana: Antología e introducción histórica.* Ed rev. 2 vols. New York: Holt, Rinehart and Winston.
Arciniegas (1970), Germán. *El continente de siete colores: Historia de la cultura en América Latina.* Buenos Aires: Editorial Sudamericana.
Baudelaire (1982), Charles. *Les Fleurs du Mal.* Trans. Richard Howard. Boston: David R. Godine.
Beckett (1985), Samuel, trans. *Mexican Poetry: An Anthology.* New York: Grove Press.
Bell (1987), Steven M. "Mexico" in Foster 1987: 329-403.
Benedetti (1992), Mario. "Temas y problemas" in Fernández Moreno 1992: 354-71.
Blackwell (1937), Alice Stone, trans. *Some Spanish-American Poets.* Ed. Isaac Goldberg. Philadelphia: University of Pennsylvania Press.
Borges (1998), Jorge Luis. *Collected Fictions.* Trans. Andrew Hurley. New York and London: Penguin Books.
Calvillo (1944), Manuel, ed. *Paisaje* by Manuel José Othón. México, DF: Universidad Nacional Autónoma de México.
Castro Leal (1974), Antonio. "Prólogo." Othón 1974.
Chang-Rodríguez (2004), Raquel and Malva E. Filer. *Voces de Hispanoamérica: Antología literaria.* 3rd ed. Boston: Thomson-Heinle.
Cuddon (1992), J.A. *The Penguin Dictionary of Literary Terms and Literary Theory.* 3rd ed. London: Penguin Books.
Díaz Mirón (1984), Salvador. *Lascas* (Jalapa, 1901). Ed. facs. México: Premiá Ed.
Diccionario de la lengua española (DLE, 2001). Real Academia Española. 2 vols. Madrid: Espasa-Calpe.

Fernández (1967), Justino. *Mexican Art*. Paul Hamlyn-The Colour Library of Art.
Fernández Moreno (1992), César. *América Latina en su literatura*. México, DF: Siglo Veintiuno Editores.
Fonseca (2010), Rodolfo. See Huidobro 2010.
Foster (1987), David William, ed. *Handbook of Latin American Literature*. New York and London: Garland Publishing.
Fuentes (1999), Carlos. *The Buried Mirror: Reflections on Spain and the New World*. Boston: Houghton-Mifflin-Mariner Books.
Gallagher (1973), D.P. *Modern Latin American Literature*. New York and Oxford: Oxford University Press.
Garganigo (2002), John F, et al. *Huellas de las literaturas hispanoamericanas*. 2nd ed. Pearson-Prentice Hall.
González Peña (1945), Carlos. *History of Mexican Literature*. Trans. Gusta Barfield Nance and Florene Johnson Dunstan. Dallas: Southern Methodist University Press.
_____ (1949). *Historia de la literatura mexicana*. 4th ed. México, DF: Editorial Porrúa.
Grossman (2010, Edith. *Why Translation Matters*. New Haven and London: Yale University Press.
Huidobro (2010), Vicente. *Acróbata del cielo*. Ed. Rodolfo Fonseca. México: Santillana-Alfaguara.
Knox (1993), Bernard, ed. *The Norton Book of Classical Literature*. New York and London: W.W. Norton.
Montejano y Aguiñaga (1997), Rafael. *Manuel José Othón y su ambiente*. San Luis Potosí: Universidad Autónoma de San Luis Potosí.
Neruda (1999), Pablo. *The Heights of Macchu Picchu*. Trans. Nathaniel Tarn. New York: Farrar, Straus and Giroux.
Othón (1902), Manuel José. *Poemas rústicos*. México, DF: Aguilar Vera y Co.
_____ (1917). *Poemas escogidos*. Ed. Agustín Loera y Chávez. México, DF: Cultura.
_____ (1944). *Paisaje*. Ed. M. Calvillo. México, DF: UNAM.
_____ (1974). *Poesías y cuentos*. Ed. Antonio Castro Leal. 3rd ed. México, DF: Editorial Porrúa.
_____ (1997). *Obras completas*. Ed. J.A. Peñalosa. 2 vols. México, DF: Fondo de Cultura Económica.

Pacheco (1999), José Emilio, Ed. *Antología de modernismo (1884-1921)*.
    México, DF: Universidad Nacional Autónoma de México—
    Ediciones Era.
Pagaza (1887), Joaquín Arcadio. *Murmurios de la selva: ensayos poéticos*.
    México, DF: Imprenta de Francisco Díaz León.
Paz (1985), Octavio, ed. *Mexican Poetry: An Anthology*. Trans. Samuel
    Beckett. New York: Grove Press.
_____ (1987). *Convergences: Essays on Art and Literature*. Trans. Helen Lane.
    New York: Harcourt Brace Jovanovich.
Peñalosa (1997), Joaquín Antonio, ed. See Othón 1997.
Preminger (1974), Alex, Frank J. Warnke and O.B. Hardison, Ed.
    Princeton Encyclopedia of Poetry and Poetics. Princeton, NJ:
    Princeton University Press.
Ramírez (2017), Fausto. *José María Velasco: pintor de paisajes*. México, DF:
    Fondo de Cultura Económica—Universidad Nacional
    Autónoma de México.
Smith (1968), Bradley. *Mexico: A History in Art*. Garden City, NY:
    Doubleday & Company.
Stavans (2011), Ilan, ed. *The FSG Book of Twentieth-Century Latin American*
    Poetry. New York: Farrar, Straus and Giroux.
Tapscott (1999), Stephen, ed. *Twentieth-Century Latin American Poetry: A*
    Bilingual Anthology. Austin: The University of Texas Press.
Torres-Rioseco (1967), Arturo. *The Epic of Latin American Literature*.
    Berkeley and Los Angeles: University of California Press.
Vallejo (2007), César. *The Complete Poetry: A Bilingual Edition*. Trans.
    Clayton Eshleman. Berkeley and Los Angeles: University of
    California Press.
Washbourne (2007), Kelly, ed. *An Anthology of Spanish American*
    Modernismo. Trans. Kelly Washbourne with Sergio Waisman.
    New York: Modern Language Association.
Zaid (2003), Gabriel, ed. *Ómnibus de poesía mexicana*. México, DF: Siglo
    Veintiuno.
Zavala (1952), Jesús. *Manuel José Othón, el hombre y el poeta*. México:
    Imprenta Universitaria.

Manuel José Othón

Born in San Luis Potosí, Mexico, in 1858, he studied classics in school, and was already translating and writing poetry as early as the mid-1870s. His first volume, *Poesías*, was published in 1880. He studied law at the Instituto Científico de San Luis Potosí, graduating in 1881. After 1883 he moved quite a bit between Mexico City, San Luis Potosí and other cities and small towns around the central and northern Mexican highlands. Lawyer, judge, and even federal legislator at one point, he continued to write poetry, drama, and fiction throughout the remainder of his life. In 1892 he was elected to the prestigious Academia Mexicana de la Lengua. Throughout the 1890s he published his poems in modernist journals such as the *Revista Azul* and *Revista Moderna*. In 1902 he published *Poemas rústicos*, which collected most of the poetry he had written between 1889 and 1901. His health failing, he returned one last time to San Luis Potosí where he died in 1906 at the age of forty-eight. Once considered to be among the great Mexican moderns, he is still unsurpassed as a poet of nature and the landscape of north-central Mexico.

José María Velasco (1840-1912; cover painting) was México's foremost landscape painter in the last half of the nineteenth century.

Julio Ruelas (1870-1907), who executed the author portrait and illustrations on pages 42, 60, 88, 120, was the artist whose illustrations often accompanied Othón's works in the *Revista Moderna*. He was responsible for at least three separate portraits of Othón.

Alexander J. McNair teaches Spanish at Baylor University where he is an associate professor in the Department of Modern Languages and Cultures. He earned his MA and PhD in Hispanic Literature from The University of Texas at Austin. His previous books, *Romancero viejo* (2006) and *Poema de Mio Cid* (2008), are annotated editions of early Spanish poetry.

www.ingramcontent.com/pod-product-compliance
Lightning Source LLC
Chambersburg PA
CBHW022116040426
42450CB00006B/725